evolution of a valley

evolution
of a
valley

the Androscoggin story

Page Helm Jones

PHOENIX PUBLISHING
Canaan, New Hampshire

Printed in the United States of America
by Courier Printing Company
Binding by New Hampshire Bindery
Design by A. L. Morris

Library of Congress Catalog Card Number 74-81953
ISBN 0-914016-16-4

CONTENTS

v

FOREWORD

The purpose of the following pages is to give in capsule form the history of a river valley, beginning in the days before the white man. This is a saga of a typical American area which, like many, has been dominated in the last century and a half by its industrial development and grew unplanned, uncharted, and uninspired, with no thought beyond the problems of the current moment. The incentive for the developers was a combination of the pioneer motto of "make do with what you have," and a desire for profit and power mixed with a portion of personal greed. These men were not philosophers but conquerors and their methods were wasteful in the extreme of natural resources which abounded in such enormous quantities that no thought was given to the distant tomorrows. It was inevitable that under such conditions the woodlands were ravaged with nothing left but stumps and brush and the convenient rivers filled with garbage and waste products. After all, the ocean was the place for such stuff, and there was all that convenient water flowage to take it there.

The results of these operations were not recognized by the populace until halfway through the present century when the word ecology came into general use. It has taken the better part of thirty years to face realistically the crisis in our environment, though there is the danger that fanaticism in solving our difficulties will bring disaster to our economy. The water pollution situation in the Androscoggin Valley was so serious in 1941 that efforts started some fifteen years ahead of most other parts of the country failed to halt the continued contamination of one of America's most beautiful streams. Whether rejuvenation will be accomplished or not will be seen in the late seventies.

This book is not intended to indict the guilty, but rather to relate how it happened, and point out what is necessary to cure the ills caused by our lack of foresight.

1

the Beginnings

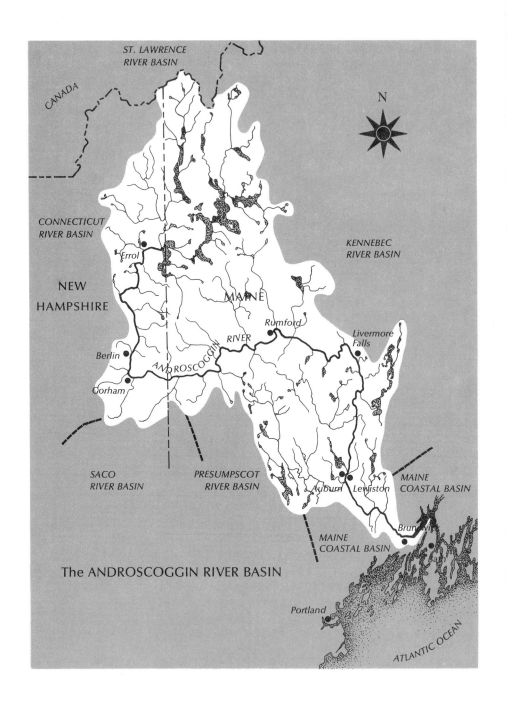

The ANDROSCOGGIN RIVER BASIN

2 / *Evolution of a Valley*

CHAPTER 1

the
Androscoggin geology

Geologists tell us that the Appalachian Mountains of the eastern United States were formed over two hundred million years ago whereas the Rockies and the Andes were not pushed up until about seventy million years ago. Thus the peaks of these later youngsters among the mountain chains would be no higher than our eastern oldsters if they had been eroding for the additional hundred and thirty million years. The real interest of the layman in the history of our eastern rivers starts just yesterday in time, during the later days of the Cenozoic era when the great polar ice cap began to melt into glaciers and the glaciers started to withdraw northward. As they moved, their billions of tons of scrapings gouged out the sloping waterways which we know today as our rivers and streams.

This geologic theory of the formation of the Androscoggin River is logical when one views a contour map. Better still, he should ascend to the peak of Mount Washington with a good pair of field glasses on a clear day and follow the valley from the Canadian line down through the edge of New Hampshire and on over into Maine to the ocean. It is apparent that the retreating glaciers left a chain of lakes from the coast near present-day Brunswick to the Canadian border of New Hampshire and Maine.

The first of these lakes was present-day Merrymeeting Bay and the last of approximately the same age were lakes Parmachenee, Aziscohos, Cupsuptic, Mooselookmeguntic, Kennebago, Rangeley, Richardson, and Umbagog. These lakes retained their approximate shapes from then on, but the others in the chain below which were of less depth, did not. As the lower lakes gradually filled with drainage water and eventually overflowed during the period after the ice had left, their outlets gradually cut into the glacier-left dams. Over the vast eras of time, estimated at some 15,000 years, these same outlets eroded deep enough to drain the lakes down to a river channel, leaving areas of rich alluvial soil in the bottom lands, or intervales as they are called in New England. These beautiful intervales are similar to those of the Connecticut and other glacier formed rivers. Before the erection of the many control and industrial dams along the Androscoggin, the valley was subject to disastrous floods each spring and even now, occasionally an extra heavy runoff, following unusually thick snow cover and quick thaw, will cause flood damage.

This partial control of water level, however, was the one and only benefit which conservationists admit has come from the industrial complexes which dot the river at Berlin, Rumford, Livermore, Lewiston, and Brunswick, and daily have dumped thousands of tons of chemical waste into what was once a fisherman's paradise. Each spring thousands of Atlantic salmon came in from the ocean and fought their way up to the very sources of the tributaries to spawn. It was the year-round home of brook trout, the size of which would stagger a modern angler, and millions of shad swam partway up each year. Near the mouth and up to the falls at present-day Lewiston, alewives invaded the tributary brooks in countless hordes. They were caught in weirs built by the Anasagunticook Indians and then smoked by the squaws for their braves to nibble on during the fierce Maine winters. These were some of the riches of the once unspoiled Androscoggin.

CHAPTER 2

sources
and boundaries

The sources of all our rivers have been controversial, but doubly so when used in determining international or even state boundaries. The little known Androscoggin River is no exception even though the name of the river does not appear in the controversy. The reason for this is that the Androscoggin is not called by that name until the junction of the Magalloway River and the outlet from Umbagog Lake at Errol, New Hampshire. Prior to that point it is called the Magalloway River. This dates back to Indian times when there were no fewer than seven sections of the river which bore distinct names. The river, from its mouth in Merrymeeting Bay to present day Lewiston, was known as the Pejepscot and sometimes Sagadahoc, above Lewiston Falls as Amitgonpotook and above Canton Point as the Aurconganunticook. Beyond Berlin and on to the junction at Errol it was called Ponticook or Pontook. Above this it was called Magalloway and retains that name to this day. The name Androscoggin was apparently an anglicized spelling of one of the sixty different translations of what the Indians themselves called the river as a whole. The most prevalent, however, was Amascoggin which could have meant "fish country in springtime" or "place of fish spearing," either of which translations would have been fitting.

The controversy over the source of the Androscoggin arose in 1783 from the very vague wording in the agreement setting the boundaries of Eastern Canada and the United States. Quoting the Treaty of Versailles, ending the American Revolution:

From the northwest angle of Nova Scotia viz., that angle which is formed by a line drawn due north from the source of St. Croix River to the Highlands which divide those rivers that empty themselves into the River St. Lawrence from those which fall into the Atlantic Ocean to the Northwestermost head of Connecticut River, then down along the middle of that river to the 45 degree of North Latitude; from thence, by a line due west on said latitude etc.

The italicized description of an unsurveyed line started a controversy which raged for thirty-six years all along the 475 mile border of the Maine territory of Massachusetts and the Canadian-New Hampshire line, as well as the state borders of Vermont, New Hampshire, and Maine.

At Ghent, Belgium, where the commissioners of both nations met in 1814 at the close of the War of 1812, the matter was somewhat clarified and at least a method of settling the disputes was arrived at as follows (From Article V, Treaty of Ghent):

Whereas neither that point of the highlands lying due North of the source of the River St. Croix and designated in the former treaty of peace between the two powers as the Northwest angle of Nova Scotia, nor the Northwestermost head of Connecticut River has yet been ascertained, and not yet been surveyed, it is agreed . . . Two commissioners shall be appointed, sworn and authorized to act—etc.

The commissioners were appointed and ran a survey line during 1817 and 1818 but somehow omitted in their report to the authorities the results of the survey, except that part of it which set the border westward from present Beecher Falls, Vermont, on the 45th degree north latitude line and its intersection with the St. Lawrence River and down that river to Lake Ontario. Probably this was because of the fact that the actual survey line ran down the dividing highlands and exact latitude and longitude readings would have been, due to the variations each few hundred feet, almost impossible. However, permanent markings were planted and the line was drawn.

The report was accepted in 1822 but bickering on the portion of the border between New Hampshire and Canada continued with much confusion over the actual line location due largely to an obstreperous colony of settlers on what they called Indian Stream which was a tributary of the Connecticut River. It was said by the respectable and law-abiding citizens of Lower Coos County, New Hampshire, that the settlement was composed of renegades from law or church, jailbreakers and felons who had escaped from the more civilized coastal regions to what they thought was across the border in British-held Canada. Actually this was somewhat inaccurate for the settlers on Indian Stream were about the same caliber as those below and felt the urge to leave the "crowded" areas the same as the settlers of lower Coos County, New Hampshire, and their characters were no different. True, they had no ties in the new State of New Hampshire and probably thought they were in Canada, but after settling they also had no liking for Canadian authority or taxes either. In a spirit of a "curse on both your houses" in July of 1832 one Luther Parker, together with assorted other Parkers, Blanchards, Terrells, and others, formally organized the Republic of Indian Stream. They adopted a written and logical constitution, elected a President who was Luther Parker, set up an assembly and courts and even authorized the coinage of Indian Stream money. The Republic existed and functioned for three years with sporadic invasions of sheriffs and tax collectors from both Canada and New Hampshire who were summarily repulsed by Parker and his supporters. There was some gunfire and a good many fisticuffs, but in 1835 the New Hampshire legislature ordered its militia into the disputed territory and caused the dissolution of the Republic. Parker, who was a born leader and a man of iron convictions, promptly gathered his goods and family and emigrated westward to the newer and less congested territory of Wisconsin where he became a leading citizen, was elected to the first territorial legislature, and his son was twice lieutenant governor of that state.

Indian Streamers originally based their claim to being Canadians on the "source" of the Connecticut River which they claimed was the Magalloway and the stream flowing from Third Lake, thus making the border come east some twenty miles on the 45th degree latitude and extending on the same line as that of Vermont. Later, when they saw that Canadian authority was equally as obnoxious as that of New Hampshire, they used the actual sources as arguments against Canadian claims, having discovered that the connection between one source brook of the Magalloway was actually separated from the source of Third Lake by a few hundred feet.

State authorities however, after the dissolution by force of the Republic, determined to settle the differences with Canada and in 1836 a committee was appointed by the New Hampshire General Court to ascertain the boundary between New Hampshire, Maine, and Lower Canada. The committee, spurred on by the now thoroughly aroused New Hampshire authorities, surveyed the sources of both the Connecticut and the Magalloway and found that they did not touch, though springs feeding both were only a hundred yards or so apart. They also decided that the main branch of the Connecticut was in truth Hall's Stream which was west of Indian Stream and that the true border should be down the middle of that stream. However, government commissions moved exceedingly slow and it was not until the Webster-Ashburton Treaty between the United States and Great Britain was signed in 1842 that the matter was settled and Hall's Stream was substituted in the wording for Connecticut River. Meantime, the source of the Androscoggin River had been mapped and surveyed, and the streams forming the Magalloway, the Cupsuptic, and the Kennebago Rivers, being the true sources of the Androscoggin, all spring from the high points of the original wording of the Versailles treaty. This sets the boundary as the height of land separating the watersheds of the St. Lawrence and rivers flowing generally south to the Atlantic Ocean.

CHAPTER 3

first citizens

. . . the Valley Indians

Of New England's rivers, the Androscoggin holds a unique place in that it is probably the least known, or least publicized, of the major rivers of the area.

Unlike the Penobscot, the Kennebec, the Saco, the Merrimack or the Connecticut, the Androscoggin was, during the great river traffic days before the railroads, unnavigable except by canoe with many carries around falls and rapids, even though it did serve as transportation for billions of feet of logs and pulpwood to its mills and to the tidewater. It drains an area of over 3,000 square miles of populated territory in Maine and New Hampshire.

The valley was, however, settled by white men much later than any of the other river valleys mentioned above and thus its written history begins much later in the eighteenth century than the others whose recorded story begins prior to 1600.

The settlement of all of New England moved inward from the coast, and the peculiar geography of the mouth of the Androscoggin contributed to its neglect for almost two centuries. The river does not flow directly into the ocean, but joins tidewater in Merrymeeting Bay — as do the bigger Kennebec and the smaller Cathance. The outlet of the bay itself, which is in truth a tidal strait, is called the Kennebec for its seventeen odd miles until it empties into the Atlantic through a cluster of islands at its mouth. Hence, the early explorers of the New England Coast, Verrazano, Champlain, Cartier, and John Smith, naturally assumed that the Kennebec was the only major river flowing into Merrymeeting Bay. It is of interest that both Verrazano (in 1524) and Champlain (in 1605) saw and noted the snowcapped White Mountains from the coast but neither followed the river which would have brought them to those mountains. Practically no mention is made in their writings of the river except by Smith, whose accounts were written in England from what must have been rather vague notes and scanty maps.

The fact is that it was remarkable that any of the early explorers of the coast actually went up into Merrymeeting Bay, for the view from the ocean of the forty miles of shoreline between Pemaquid Point and Casco Bay is, even now, with excellent charts and instruments for guidance, a baffling and confusing prospect for any but the most skillful navigators. This is due to the seven openings which look very much alike and can easily be mistaken for each other. They are the Johns River and Bay, Damariscotta River, the Sheepscot River, the Kennebec, the New Meadows River, Harpswell Sound, and Middle Bay. All except the Kennebec peter out into small brooks after a few miles, and the Kennebec itself looks very much as if it will disappear also just above present-day Bath. This is due to a multiplicity of small islands and channels in the two-mile stretch just prior to the narrow entrance to the bay. The entrance is called the Chops, which on an ebbing tide is a raging hundred yards of foaming fury.

Nevertheless, in 1614 John Smith did move into the bay and possibly up the Androscoggin. He writes, "Up this river at Amuckcawgen, Kinnebeck, and Divers others, where there is planted some corn fields." He goes on later however, "Along this river 40 or 50 miles I saw nothing but great high cliffs of barren rocks, overgrown with woods," which certainly described the Kennebec and not the Androscoggin.

Champlain had earlier, in 1605, mentioned entering Merrymeeting Bay and said, "Here descend two rivers, the Quimbequg (Kennebec) which comes from the northeast and another which comes from the northwest by which Marchim and Sazinov were to come, but having watched the whole of this day without seeing them we . . . came to the mouth of the river." It is not known who Marchim and Sazinov were, but it is assumed that they were Anasagunticooks who occupied the Androscoggin Valley and it can also be assumed that Champlain did not go up the river itself. Even on his later voyages, when he may have ascended the Kennebec to the present site of Augusta, he still did not mention the Androscoggin.

In 1600 the Androscoggin Valley was the home of the Anasagunticook Indians who were of the Algonquin family and Abanakis of the four tribes of that branch in Maine. They were closer to the Canabis of the Kennebec in relations and alliances but were also friendly with the Sokokis of New Hampshire and the Picatoquos of lower Casco Bay. They were, however, as was true of the other Maine tribes, not friendly with the Tarratines of the Penobscot. In fact, that tribe seemed to be in a perpetual cold war with the other Maine tribes. By and large, however, the New England tribes tended to be isolationists in their own valleys until after the white man had threatened their existence. The country was so vast and abounding in game and fish that the tribes probably were more at peace with each other than any of the several nations in northeastern America. There were no such internecine wars as those between the Hurons and the Iroquois and except for some long-past invasions from New York of Mohawks against the Indians of the Connecticut Valley and the Pentooks of New Hampshire, the northern New England Indians were much more peaceful than otherwise. There was a coolness between the Tarratines in the great valley of the Penobscot and the coast and southern valley Indians, but it was not serious. The economics of the various valleys did not cause much inter-tribal friction as the valleys of the Penobscot, Kennebec, Androscoggin, Saco, and Merrimac were quite sufficient for hunting, fishing, and the agronomy of each tribe.

The Anasagunticooks were perhaps more isolationists than the others, for their country, the entire valley from the sources to Merrymeeting Bay, were economically self-sufficient, bound on each side by high hills and mountains for most of its length. These highlands more or less served the same purpose as the Atlantic and Pacific Oceans did for the United States until the twentieth century. The Anasagunticooks were not interested in foreign entanglements and except for loose alliances with neighboring tribes they were isolationists until the white man's threat gave them common cause for defense.

From all of the data which we have been able to gather, which is mostly folklore and tales handed down from father to son in families of the very earliest settlers of the valley, the tribe was comparatively higher in intellect, physical well-being, and tribal citizenship than most of the other Abanaki tribes. Whether this was because of their isolation or lack of warlike activities it is hard to say, but they managed their economy surprisingly well in a country surrounded by all the hazards of the primeval forest where winters were bitterly cold and the growing season was short.

The tribe was nomadic to the extent that they had no permanent year-round homes, though their villages were located in the same places permanently. Whether, however, they maintained the lodges all year or rebuilt them when they came back is not known. The largest of their settlements and probably the most permanent was at Canton Point where they had their largest cultivated plots of the rich intervale land. Here they planted their maize in early June and the women who did all of the manual labor in agronomy and in the household, lived with the old men and small children from early spring until late fall. Here too the summer harvests were stored for the bleak winter months. Meantime the hunters and trappers ranged far and wide up the entire length of the valley, touching base back at headquarters at Canton Point with heavily-loaded canoes containing deer and moose meat for smoking and animal hides in bales for winter robes and wigwam shelter covers. In late fall, when the river and lakes were frozen hard, practically the entire tribe would migrate downriver to their winter village sites on the fingers which jut out into the ocean below Brunswick. Here the weather was much milder due to the gulf stream, and living was easier in the bitter months with fishing possible, to some extent, in Casco Bay which rarely froze.

In the spring when the ice went out of the river the exodus upriver began, and each of the numerous lodge sites, including the big one at Canton, would be occupied by groups of varying sizes for the work to be done. Children, squaws, and oldsters stayed at permanent camp-sites, such as Canton Point and Laurel Hill (present-day Auburn), and the braves at the fishing camps near all of the great falls and cascades of the river.

Most of these fishing camps, as distinguished from the villages which were placed at spots suitable for planting (the intervales), were adjacent to the rapids and falls of the river where the spearing of big fish was made possible as the salmon and sturgeon migrated in their leaping climb of the falls and cataracts. Thus at Brunswick Falls which the Indians called Pejepscot, and at Lewiston (Amitgonpotook), at Livermore (Rocomocko), and Rumford; while above Bethel again we find evidence of village and agricultural life but not quite on the scale of the settlement at Canton where, according to Latham, there were 500 acres cleared and planted.

During the spring fish migration the fishing camps were usually occupied by braves with a few squaws for the household duties and the smoking of fish for later use. Fishing was not a sport for grown-ups, but rather a serious harvesting of food so that after an Indian passed into manhood, when about fifteen, he confined his fishing to spearing the big salmon and sturgeon, except when he was hunting and wanted the succulent smaller fish for a needed meal. Then he would angle in the nearby brook for trout with alder pole, sinew line, and a hook of fish bone baited with a grub worm from the nearby bank, or with a grasshopper impaled. He was a competent angler, for the fishing by line and hook was the summer occupation of all small Indian boys and girls in the Androscoggin Valley and it is quite possible that even the grown-up warrior who had put childish games away got a small thrill when he pulled out a fat two-pound squaretail, though it was the women and children who furnished the small fresh fish and farm products. By and large the adult male was a hunter, spearer, and when necessary, warrior; his providing was largely a matter of heavy meat and furs and hides for the women to make into garments and footwear. The men made the weapons and heavy utensils.

The governing of the tribe was simple and quite democratic and served the purpose well. There was practically no crime existent in the valley, mainly because there was no such thing as private property, even to the personal weapons and ornaments of the individual, which were held by them on condition of good behavior and ability. The supreme ruler was the Sagamore whose headquarters were at Canton Point. He was elected for life and the final decision on all matters was his. His council consisted of the Sachems or Chiefs and evidently there was an indeterminate number of these leaders, but it is assumed by most authorities that they too were elected by their own followers and acted as leaders in their own sub-tribe or community, while all matters affecting the whole tribe were discussed in a council of Sachems presided over by the Chief Sagamore. Monogamy was usual though there were instances where a chief maintained more than one wife. They were a light-hearted and happy people who had adjusted over the generations to their rugged land and were content with their isolation. Their dealings with the neighboring tribes, while infrequent, were cordial. About once a year there was a gathering of Sachems from several of the tribes including the Canabis of the Kennebec, the Piscataquis, and the Sokokis of the Saco to discuss their common problems. This was held somewhere on Casco Bay and it was no doubt at one of these sessions that the word of the kidnapping of Wawanock braves by George Weymouth in 1605 was received by the Anasagunticooks and the first dread planted of the danger to their way of life in their beloved valley. There had been rumors of the strange white creatures who had touched the coast in their enormous canoes, but these had excited nothing but curiosity, untinged with suspicion. This, however, was different and the Sagamore and Sachems were on guard for the time when their own land would be invaded by strangers.

Early in the 17th century the idyllic life of the Indians of the valley began to change because of this suspicion of the white invaders and their growing numbers on the coast below and above the mouth of the river. In 1607 there occurred the first recorded actual contact with white men. Captain Gilbert of the ill-fated Popham colony skirted the shores of Merrymeeting Bay and rowed up the Androscoggin River where a few miles above Brunswick he was met by a small party of Indians under Sachem Sabeona in a canoe. After circling each other suspiciously like strange dogs, they entered into negotiations by sign language and after exchanging the chief for one of Gilbert's men in each craft, they proceeded up the river, the longboat following the canoe. Some of the Englishmen actually visited an Indian camp a short way inland where were gathered some several hundred warriors, armed and in full war paint. It was apparently an unsatisfactory conference with suspicion on both sides, and violence was narrowly averted before the English got safely downstream. This was the first recorded naming of an Anasagunticook Indian, this Sachem Sabeona, who was afterwards Chief Sagamore of the tribe and was apparently the forefather of a long line of Chiefs called Sabattus.

The period between 1607 and 1628, as far as Indian lore is concerned, is shrouded in mystery except for the fairly well-established fact that during this period, and it is agreed by most of the early authorities that the year was 1615, plague broke out among the Anasagunticooks of the valley and decimated the tribe. What this plague was, no one seems to have any idea, as no white man recorded the symptoms or the type of illness brought on. Modern authorities have theorized that it was a virulent influenza or possibly smallpox or even the bubonic plague. The latter theory has some basis of fact for there was a catastrophic epidemic in London in 1603 and it is plausible that infested rats could have been brought over in English ships with their carrier fleas and transmitted to the rodents native to New England. Too, there were cases reported in Massachusetts Colony ports during the period. But the only recorded facts of the 'Sagunticook plague were that the disease killed the tribe like flies and reduced the total number of warriors above sixteen from several thousand to less than fifteen hundred in the entire valley, and the mortality rate among the young, the very old, and the women must have been even greater.

The effect of this disaster on the tribe cannot be measured nor the effect on the attitude toward the whites, for it has been thought by most authorities that the medicine men of the tribe, being confronted by a catastrophe which they were incapable of handling, had blamed the rumored white invasion of the coast with the introduction of the disease. In fact, it is probable that this was the first accusation of germ warfare made in history, though it was indicated as witchcraft or a supernatural curse rather than germicidal.

Whatever the plague was and whatever the Indians blamed for the disaster it apparently did immediately affect their tribal policies and their mode of life for it was about this time that they began to abandon their camp and village sites near the coast and make certain other moves toward defending their river against the English. A village at Mere Point was abandoned. The one at Maquoit and Pejepscot (Brunswick), and over the next few years the villages at present Lisbon Falls, the mouth of the Sabattus River, and in fact all settlements below Lewiston Falls, were moved to a newly established strong point built at the mouth of the Little Androscoggin River on Laurel Hill in present-day New Auburn.

In 1628 Thomas Purchase (spelled Purchas in some records) was granted a small tract of land on the river at the present site of Brunswick and he soon settled there, building a fortified home and trading post. He was the first Englishman to actually live on the Androscoggin and he had a definite part in the later relations of the settlers with the

Indians. Little is known of the man except the bare fact of his occupation of the post and of his extensive trade with the Indians. Through him they were first introduced to "fire water" and later claimed that Purchase was a cheat, a liar, and the Indians' worst enemy, though they continued to trade with him for the length of his stay on the river. In 1632 Purchase and George Way received a patent of tremendous size on each side of the river and while Way never settled there, Purchase continued his trade activity. In 1639 he conveyed part of the land to Governor John Winthrop and members of the "Governor and Company of the Massachusetts Bay in New England," and thereafter moved his operation further upriver. There is no further recorded mention of this man until 1675 and then it is to be presumed that the Thomas Purchas referred to must be a descendant of the original one for he would have been in his eighties which would have made unlikely his being active in trade and family raising in those times.

Other traders had now joined Purchase and the Anasagunticook Sachems began to sell land to the newcomers though no permanent settlement of these lands appeared for some years. Why the Sachems who previously had no knowledge of property rights did this is not known, but it is assumed that this very lack of any idea of values was the reason the traders were able to make what were ridiculous deals. The Indians thought that they were getting the best of the white invaders as they always insisted that they retain hunting and fishing rights on their land. This, they felt, protected them, since they could see no reason for the actual ownership of the land having anything to do with the situation. In fact, they thought they were receiving value for nothing and were making very sharp trades, though the rum, pots, pans, and cheap tools were as laughable as the pittance involved in the trade for Manhattan Island by the Dutch.

The relations with the English during the middle seventeenth century created a steadily mounting resentment among the Anasagunticooks which, by comparison with their contact with the French, rare though it was, was most cordial. The Canabis of the Kennebec were the closest of any other tribe to the Anasagunticooks and they had often been visited by the French priests and traders by way of the northern sources of the Kennebec River. These contacts had created a very friendly relationship with the French as compared to that with the English. The French, whose first penetrations of the Maine wilderness were made by Jesuit priests, had been most sympathetic toward the Indians, in contrast with the English whose attitude was that of conqueror of very inferior beings. The Jesuits were cordially received and many converts were made among the Canabis. Even the French traders were more readily accepted by the tribes and their reputations for fair barter were rarely protested. The reason for this difference was obviously the difference in aims of the two peoples. The English were primarily interested in the acquisition of land and the planting of permanent settlements. On the other hand the French priests were interested in the salvation of souls among the benighted, and the traders in the well-being of the Indians in order that they might continue successfully to trap and hunt furbearing animals for trade with the French.

The English felt that the sooner they got rid of the troublesome aborigines the better, while the Frenchman's aim was to aid the well-being of the Indians with a view to a much longer range development of the new land.

It is uncertain how much actual contact the Anasagunticooks had with the French, though relations at the northern end of their valley were existent to some extent, for the Frenchmen were roaming all of southern Quebec and in fact down the Hudson, Seneca, and Genesee Valleys. It is probable, too, that Father Paul LeJeune may have visited the valley in 1633-34 when he wintered in Maine with Montegais. In 1646 Father Gabriel Druilettes followed what became later the Arnold route from Quebec down to Augusta on the Kennebec and possibly diverted over into the Androscoggin Valley and converted some of the tribesmen. Again in 1650 he came down into central Maine and while his writings did not mention the Androscoggin by name, he did indicate some westward wanderings and conversions of the natives. Then there were the visits of the Brothers Vincent and Jaques Bigot and, in 1689, Father Sebastian Rasles was in the neighborhood.

Regardless of the scarcity of actual contact, the influence of the French was felt by the valley Indians to such an extent that the animosity toward the English was increased and when the end finally came, it was the French offer of sanctuary at St. Francis that the Anasagunticooks accepted when they left the Androscoggin forever.

It is fairly apparent that during the years between 1640 and 1670 there was very little movement of settlers up the Androscoggin, but there is record of land sales by various Sagamores of the tribe to the English, beginning with the islands and sea-thrust necks of land below Brunswick which the Indians had abandoned. There is record of three Englishmen settling at Topsham in 1669 after purchase of land from two Anasagunticook Sachems. The settlers were Thomas Gyles, James Thomas, and Samuel York. It is also apparent that there were others besides those mentioned in recorded deeds who had begun to move up the river. There were the King's men who had already begun their ranging upriver and blazing with the King's mark the tall pines for masts of the Royal Navy. All of this activity must have filled the Indians with grave misgivings and strengthened the alliances for war which the Canabis and Sokokis had been urging. These two tribes had already been more exposed to the English than the Anasagunticooks and they had tales of mistreatment which the Androscoggin Indians could not ignore. War fever had been growing in the tribe during these years, and when the King James War broke out in 1675 against the Plymouth colony and spread northward rapidly, Tarumkin, who was at that time Chief Sagamore of the tribe at Canton Point, dispatched war parties to join the other tribes. These men were present in all of the raids which took place on the coastal settlements and were said to be the fiercest and most cruel of the warriors. They were, however, peculiarly merciful in their depredations against the settlers in their own valley, as demonstrated by their first raid in September of 1675 on the trading post of Thomas Purchase who, as previously noted, was probably the son of the original Purchase.

Here, though Purchase was absent himself, the women and children were spared though the post was burned. This raid on Purchase and a later one on Thomas Wakely nearby were apparently the only actions recorded as taking place on the Androscoggin during the period of this first Indian war, but there is evidence that Anasagunticooks were present and participated in raids at Saco, Scarboro, Wells, Berwick, and Salmon Falls, and during this period there was much killing and burning. In August, 1676, the trading post of Richard Hammond on Merrymeeting Bay was raided and three killed and sixteen whites taken into captivity. On Arrosec Island, across from present-day Bath, the trading post of Clark and Lake was raided by this same party of braves and thirty-five persons were either killed or taken prisoner.

The war continued furiously with lightning raids on settlements up and down the coast and with retaliatory action by the English which served to enrage the Abanakis. One of these inflammatory, and in this case shameful, deeds of the English was the disgraceful treachery of Major Waldron when he attacked a large group of Indians present for a peace parley at Dover, where over two-hundred Indians, many of them Anasagunticooks, were either slain or taken into captivity and sold as slaves. The use by the English of Mohawk hirelings from New York, hereditary enemies of the Abanaki, in raids against the Saco Indians was also inflammatory and, while the whites of the coast were taking an unmerciful beating, it was a war of attrition for the Anasagunticooks and in 1678 they proposed peace to the English. At the meeting with the English and the signing of the Treaty of Peace, Tarumkin, Chief Sagamore of the Anasagunticooks, was the spokesman for the Abanaki and one of the signers of the treaty. However, it was noted that he had been the chief advocate of war in 1675.

For the next few years the Indians and whites were at peace and settlers began to creep up the Androscoggin after Richard Wharton acquired the land of Purchase and Way from their heirs in 1683. This purchase was ratified by a deed from seven Anasagunticook Sachems: Warumbee, Darumkin, Wehikermett, Wedon, Homohegan, Nenongassett and Nimbanewett. The wording of the conveyance was interesting in that it showed the Sachems had not yet seen the peril of selling their land to the English. In the agreement Wharton was granted all "Priveleges and profits," the Indians reserving the right to improve "our ancient planting grounds" and to hunt and fish "for our own provision so long as no damage shall be done to the English 'fisery.'" The deed set the area from the seacoast to the "uppermost falls in the said Andros Coggin River" and included land on both sides of the river extending on the east side to the Kennebec River. The wording was to cause squabbles over land titles for generations.

The next ten years were peaceful between the Indians and the English and needfully so, for the Anasagunticooks had taken terrible losses in manpower during their prosecution of a war outside of their own country and scattered up and down the coast for a distance of a hundred miles. They were therefore glad to retire to their valley and lick their wounds, rebuild their supplies and equipment, recultivate their land, and suspiciously watch the incoming tide of settlement again coming up the coast.

The Mohawk allies of the English, however, did not keep the peace and partially due to pressure in their own areas now began a series of raids into Abanaki country, raids so harassing to the Pennacooks of the upper Saco Valley that Kankamagus, their Sagamore, accepted the offer of Tarumkin and the Sachems of the Anasagunticooks and moved his whole tribe to Canton Point and joined the 'Sagunticooks as Sachem of his sub-tribe. The Androscoggin Sagamore was glad of this as it gave the whole tribe a much-needed boost in its manpower.

Meantime, during the first five years of the peace, white settlements in the coastal region from Casco Bay up to Pemaquid Point had become so numerous that the Wawanocks of the coast had been pushed out of their homeland and they too accepted sanctuary from the 'Sagunticooks and joined them at Canton. Thus, by their own industry and the fortunate union of other tribes, the Androscoggin Indians had, by 1688, regained their strength and resolution to resist the English and were cocked and primed for the outbreak of the second, or King William's War.

The French had not been idle during this period and had exerted growing influence on the Maine Indians so that when Baron de Castine began his attacks up the coast all Maine tribes, including the Anasagunticooks, were unified in their resolution to destroy the English.

Now began again the same type of war for the valley tribe, raids pillaging settlements on the coast, though they were now fiercer and more devastating for the English colonists. In 1689 they captured forts at Pemaquid, New Castle, and Falmouth, and killed and burned all along the coast between those points. They burned Dover, and their successes were so elating that they became even more daring and took on more territory for their activities. Several hundred warriors, mostly from the Leeds sub-tribe of Caghnaugas, joined the French under D'Aillebout, DeMantel, and LeMoyne and invaded New York, destroying English settlements. In 1690 Schenectady was raided and burned.

In the spring of 1690 the tribe captured Fort Andros at Brunswick, Maine, it having been erected only the previous year by Governor Andros. The Indians held the fort until the fall when Colonel Church arrived with an expedition which the aroused General Court of Massachusetts had dispatched against the Indians with orders to "sail Eastward by the first opportunity to Casco or places adjacent" and to "visit the enemy, French and Indians at their headquarters at Ameras-cogen, Pejepscot or any other plat . . . killing, destroying and utterly rooting out the enemy also as much as can be done to redeeming or recovering of our captives in any place." The good colonel, however, did not accomplish any of these objectives. Indian reconnaissance was much too good. The colonel landed his strong force at Maquoit, marched to Fort Andros and found the place deserted. He then went up the river as far as the fortified camp at Laurel Hill where he discovered his first Indians, a few old men and some squaws. He destroyed the camp along with the stored grain and fish and went back to the coast, then eastward seeking the Indians. He found none and returned to Boston having accomplished nothing but the destruction of one village and its stores.

The war dragged on with occasional raids on the only settlements left in Maine, York, Wells, Kittery, and the Isle of Shoals, though little was achieved on either side except that the Indians were victorious in that they had stopped the creeping settlement. Both sides were weary of the struggle, however, and peace talks began as early as 1693. Six long years of occasional outbursts of violence and long periods of quiet were to follow in a kind of uneasy peace until the treaty was finally ratified at Mere Point in 1699 by Sagamores of all four remaining tribes of Abanakis, the Anasagunticooks, the Sokokis, the Canabis, the Tarratines and the English Commissioners.

The eleven years of hostility had been disastrous to the valley Indians, their manpower terribly depleted and their spirit weakened. They had won their war but they were losing the peace for, like an incoming tide after low ebb, the settlers were returning to their burned homes and were busy rebuilding and replanting all along the coast. The tribe had abandoned the river below Canton and it seemed that the war spirit was dead. There were several conferences with the English over the terms of the treaties; one in 1703 with Governor Dudley at Casco Bay was also attended by the French priest, Father Rasles. The Sachems were unable to cope with the English double-talk and the first movements of part of the tribe to Canada began in the period of 1703-10. Though the last of the tribe did not leave the Canton Point area until 1760, the exodus from their age-old valley homes had begun with the abandonment of the burial grounds near Lewiston Falls.

In Queen Anne's War, which took place in 1703 and lasted until 1713, there was no activity on the Androscoggin River and how many warriors of the tribe took part in the French actions is unknown, but that some did is fairly well established, for Father Rasles who had great influence, had visited them just prior to the outbreak. The good father was to be a "thorn in the side" of the English until August, 1724, when he was killed at Norridgewock. The treaty signed at the end of the war in 1714, however, did contain the names of several Anasagunticook Sachems as well as Kankamagus, the then Chief Sagamore, so the tribe must have furnished expeditionary forces to their French allies.

Again in the fourth Indian War of 1722-25, while no action took place in the valley itself except for some scattered individual raids, the signers of the treaty in 1727 were again prominently Anasagunticooks including Sabatis, the Chief Sagamore. Some authorities insist that the valley Indians were the instigators, along with the French, of both outbreaks of hostilities.

On the whole the dawn of the 18th century was the end of the Anasagunticooks as a power in the Androscoggin Valley and in Maine. From 1730 to 1760 there was a definite movement of the tribe, bag and baggage, to the upper reaches of the river and into Canada to join the St. Francis Indians, so called. The huge settlement of St. Francis, Quebec, was composed of Maine Indians from the Canabis, Sokokis and Tarratines as well as the remnants of the Anasagunticooks, all of whom had been driven from their ancestral homes by the English.

2

the River

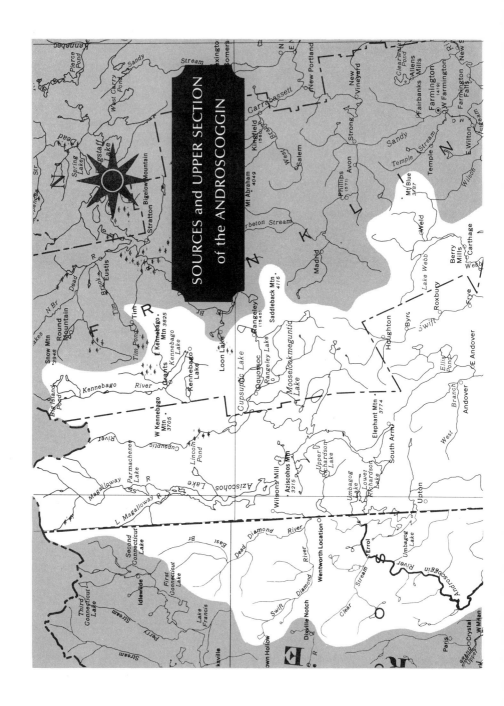

SOURCES and UPPER SECTION
of the ANDROSCOGGIN

CHAPTER 4

the

Magalloway

The international boundary line, near the junction of New Hampshire and Maine, juts up into Canada in an area of about seven by fifteen miles in Maine and contains most of the source brooks of the Magalloway which are mainly formed on slopes of the boundary ridge in nine ponds whose outlets become four named streams. First East Branch Magalloway River, Second East, Third East, and the West Branch which finally get together about six miles below the border as the Magalloway River. Here it flows about two miles before it goes into Parmachenee Lake. This stretch, and up all of the branches for that matter, is famous fishing water where two Presidents of the United States enjoyed publicized outings some years apart.

Grover Cleveland fished the stream a number of times and Dwight D. Eisenhower, during his first term, caught trout and land-locked salmon in the stream and below Little Boy Falls just above the inlet to Parmachenee Lake. Both Presidents lodged at the famous Parmachenee Club which sits on an island in the lake. The lake itself is famed for its landlocked salmon and the Parmachenee Belle, a trout fly of long-standing popularity with fly fishermen. Parmachenee is a small but deep lake about three miles in length and varying in width from a half to three-quarters of a mile, then its outlet roars down a rocky bed for about three miles where it joins the Little Magalloway River which has come in from the New Hampshire-Maine border and the crest of Rump Mountain which rears its head some 3600 feet above sea level. Here the two streams form Aziscohos Lake, a beautiful woodland body of water some fifteen miles in length. Aziscohos is largely man-made in that there is a storage dam at its outlet which makes its contour about what the original lake must have been at the end of the glacial age. The slope from the border to this point on the Magalloway varies from 3600 feet above sea level to 1500 feet or a drop of approximately 2000 feet in about thirty-five miles. Some ichthyologists believe that the landlocked salmon of Parmachenee and other upland lakes were originally trapped in those lakes when they were being formed at the end of the glacial period, while others claim they were planted by man and were not migrating Atlantics; but the fact remains that the two species are so nearly alike, except in size, that it is reasonable to believe that they had a common origin.

A canoe trip beginning at the Canadian border today and following down stream to Aziscohos Dam would be almost identical to the trip made by Indians in birchbark canoes three hundred years ago, for the area is still almost as untouched by man as it was then. True, the timber has been cut but the second growth is now almost as verdant as it was in Indian days. It is still timberland and untouched by settlers and except for the rambling buildings of the Parmachenee Club and occasional woods camps, there are no signs of man's occupancy. The whole area is controlled by the big paper concern, Brown Company of Berlin, New Hampshire, and they are carefully following what they consider the best methods of tree farming and sectional cutting in order to maintain their supply of pulpwood. Unlike the Rangeley area of lakes and streams, there are practically no summer camps on the stream or on Parmachenee or Aziscohos, for the paper company has zealously guarded the woodlands against such incursions. Even the club is an exclusive resort, open only for a few weeks of the year for the benefit of the company directors, officers, and friends.

The gates to the region near Aziscohos Dam are kept closed for entrance to the private roads except for company equipment and bearers of passes from the executive in charge of woodlands.

Below Brown Company gates, however, the scenery changes. For all of the twelve (or fifteen by canoe) miles to the junction with the other major tributaries at Errol, the river meanders through lush countryside of cultivated flat lands as it passes the first of the drained lakes or intervale areas. At this point the river edges over the state line into New Hampshire. The river is deep and slow (by comparison) as the drop in altitude, unlike most of the valley above, is but two hundred feet for the fifteen miles. Farms line the river on both sides with stretches of marshy swale punctuating the planted ground.

The river flows past the little settlement of Wilsons Mills, Maine, and down to the junction with the Diamond River at Wentworth Location, New Hampshire. This tributary is a combination of the Dead Diamond and the Swift Diamond Rivers which come in from the northwest just above the small settlement of Wentworth. The river during this sojourn of a dozen miles makes gyrations of curves and curlicues which, when one first looks at the map, are really unbelievable. There are even figures eight and complete circles, and if it were not for the highway which is in sight nearby, one could easily, by taking a wrong turn, find himself headed back upstream over the same course he paddled down just moments ago.

At its marshy mouth, in fact at the end of the Magalloway, it joins in three separate places the outlets of Lake Umbagog in what is called Leonard Pond, which is no pond at all but a confusion of narrow channels flowing in every direction of the compass and finally running off in a main stream as the Androscoggin River. In our canoe, if we have managed to follow the biggest volume of water, and this is no easy task, we now find ourselves paddling the first three miles of the river to Errol dam.

Summer on the upper tributaries of the
Androscoggin. These are gentle, winding streams . . .
a fisherman's idyll and a nature lover's paradise under
the summer sun.

CHAPTER 5

the

Rangeley Lakes'

sources

About a quarter of a mile east of the tiny pond which is the source of First East Branch of the Magalloway River on the south slope of Gosford Mountain, a 3800 foot peak on the Canadian line, there gushes a spring which is the uppermost source of the Cupsuptic River. This is the middle major source tributary of the Androscoggin. Now jump east a half-mile and three miles north where lies Massachusetts Bog, a shallow three-mile lake at the foot of the eastern slope of this same Gosford Mountain, and one finds the source of the Kennebago River, the easternmost of the major tributaries of the Androscoggin River.

These two streams, the Cupsuptic and the Kennebago, flow south parallel and separated by a range of mountains called the Kennebago Divide, and both empty into what really is Lake Mooselookmeguntic but is called Lake Cupsuptic on its northern arm. Here too empties the little two-mile long Rangeley River, the outlet of Rangeley Lake which stretches about eight miles easterly. Mooselookmeguntic extends south and covers an area of some twenty-five square miles and is connected on its west side with Richardson Lake. This lake is approximately fifteen miles in length and is narrow, being a mile to two miles wide and having an outlet at its lower west side into a stream which flows through a small deep pond appropriately called "Pond in the River." It then flows into five miles of fast water called Rapid River and into Lake Umbagog, the last of the string of lakes in the so-called Rangeley watershed. Umbagog is approximately ten square miles in area and on its west bank is an outlet which becomes immediately the Androscoggin River at Errol, New Hampshire, the state line having bisected the lake. At this same point, flowing in from the north, comes our old friend the Magalloway River.

The eastern tributary, the Kennebago, was a famous Indian route to Canada and the settlement at St. Francis where the Androscoggin Indians finally settled after being forced out of their valley. The trip was made up through the string of lakes and up the Kennebago by canoe. There was a short carrying place from the head of Massachusetts Bog to Arnold Pond and into a stream feeding Lake Megantic, and another to Indian River and into Lake St. Francis. These carries are still in evidence and a rugged canoeist even now can make the trip. This writer has been over most of this route by canoe at a time when he was much younger.

Here again there has been little change in the scenery for three hundred years until one arrives at the lower reaches of the Kennebago River where Kennebago Lake empties into the stream and here sporting camps and a well-graded road line the river bank.

The trip down the lakes to the junction with the Magalloway can be a memorable one and if you are a camera bug it is doubtful you could have enough film to do justice to the magnificence of the vistas of beautiful mountain-lake scenery. This is particularly true if the trip is made in the autumn. The colors of the surrounding mountains reflected in the lake water are indescribable. We would bypass Rangeley Lake itself on this trip though the famous resort area is also scenic to a great degree and as we paddle down the upper part of Mooselookmeguntic her western shoreline is also dotted with cottages and camps for the first several miles. However, as one approaches the narrow middle of the lake we are again in virgin wilderness, and until we arrive at the first carrying point at Upper Dam where the outlet goes into Richardson, we again might be making the trip in an Indian birchbark canoe. We pull out here and carry our canoe around the dam and resume our course down Upper Richardson past what appears to be virgin forest, down through the narrows with Metallak Mountain towering 3,000 feet above on the left and Moose Mountain on the right and into widening Lower Richardson to Middle Dam, our second portage point. We carry around the dam and put into the outlet and into Pond in the River, a little jewel of water, then after a short portage around Lower Dam, we go into the rushing rapids of well-named Rapid River.

This part of the canoe trip is figurative, because although the stretch might be negotiated by experts no average sportsman would attempt it. The usual way is to extend the portage by truck to a landing on Umbagog Lake. There is a two-hundred-foot drop between Richardson and Umbagog within a distance of about five miles, and although a few daring kayakers do run the rapids occasionally, it is extremely dangerous and practically impossible to achieve in an open canoe.

Following our figurative dash down to the calm of Umbagog Lake, one would cross the state line which bisects the body of water, continue into New Hampshire, and on to the junction with the Magalloway on the west bank of the lake. Here we join our other canoe route from Canada and proceed down the Androscoggin to Errol Dam. This is another of our water control dams (formerly for lumbering and waterpower for grist and sawmills) and is a few hundred yards above Errol Village where Route 16, north and south, is joined by Route 26 which goes west to Dixville and Colebrook and the Connecticut River. The road runs from Errol along Clear Stream which goes into the Androscoggin just below the village.

Errol itself is a tiny rural village whose one industry is forestry. It has been thus since time immemorial and its population has been practically the same for all of these years and composed of woodsmen, and now, mechanical operators of woodcutting and moving equipment. It is the last outpost of "civilian" life before entering the vast woods reserves of the paper company.

At 13 Mile Woods late winter still grips the
countryside as the icy river flows past boom pilings
formerly used for pulp wood storage.

CHAPTER 6

the

Pontook section

The river flows through the village of Errol and again leaves inhabited land as it winds through what is known as the Thirteen Mile Woods, the banks sloping on each side up to mountain ridges that parallel the valley. Here, punctuated by rapids, we find stretches of comparatively calm, slow-moving water which was formerly used by the paper company as tremendous reservoirs for softwood pulp logs. Hardwood was transported by truck as it is not buoyant enough, but since 1961 all wood is trucked to the mill. Prior to this, however, at certain times of the year it was impossible to see the surface of the water as thousands of cords of pulpwood stretched for miles from bank to bank. From time to time log booms strung across the river on steel cables separated stretches of water above the rapids so that pulpwood could be released as needed at the mills downstream at Berlin. The booms also prevented troublesome jams and pileups.

These huge, unattached rafts of floating pulpwood made navigation almost impossible except by the hard work of two men in a canoe or bateau poling the short sticks apart and going through a foot or two at a time. The short pulpwood log does not have enough buoyancy to support a man, so if one wanted to cross the river, which wood scalers who keep track of the amount of cordage in each raft must do, it was necessary to go to the bottom of the batch and cross on the log booms. A few years ago one enterprising scaler solved this difficulty in a novel way. He simply brought up an old pair of skis and wore them whenever he wanted to cross a pulpwood pond. He was then constantly supported by not one, but four or five sticks. Inasmuch as this is real ski country and almost every youngster skis before he reaches his teens, it was natural that someone would discover this summer use of the long boards, but when enquiring about it the author was assured that no one would use his good skis for this purpose. "Ruin the edges, so we just use discards," his informant told him contemptuously.

Below Thirteen Mile Woods we again come into settled countryside with pastures and cultivated land lining the river bank, and broad, flat stretches of swale grass as the river enters another Cenozoic lake. This one is Pontook Basin or as it was once called, Ponticook. The basin is formed by water partially backed up by the remains of a low dam once used by one of the paper companies for lumbering but abandoned since 1951.

For several years prior to 1967 there was considerable survey activity connected with proposals for building a high level "multipurpose" dam by either the Army Corps of Engineers or private power interests, but there were many objections from conservationists and others. In the spring of 1967 both the power company and the Army Engineers announced their decision to abandon both projects as being "too costly," though most citizens of Coos County believed the decision was politically inspired.

Beyond Holt Hill and several miles of fast water below the dam site, the river enters what was the original lake formed above Berlin Falls and which is now bottomland of a quarter to a half-mile in width on each side before rising sharply into hills and maintaining the characteristic valley formation of most of the entire length of the Androscoggin. Now both banks, and particularly the west bank, are beginning to be heavily settled. Farms and little groups of dwellings dot the roadside of Highway 16 which has followed the river bank all the way down from Errol. Five miles or so below Pontook Dam the river flows through the village of Milan, in reality a suburb of the city of Berlin, though a separate town, as is the custom in New England. Actually it is a prosperous little village whose citizens, for the most part, commute daily the six miles or so to the mills in Berlin. Those who do not are mostly woodsmen or farmers.

Across the river from Milan, built on the intervale, is the Berlin airport. Here for some years Northeast Airlines landed summer scheduled flights from Boston, and here Berlin citizens have been fighting for year-round service from both Boston and Canada. At this writing the latter apparently is dependent upon the establishment of a port of entry by the federal government.

Below Milan on the right side of the River Road one passes the Berlin Ski Jump of the Nansen Ski Club, a terrifying steel framework structure which is the site each February or March of jump meets of national and international importance. In summer the structure looks like an abandoned mine tipple on the side of the mountain.

The Nansen Ski Club was founded in 1872 by a group of Berlin Scandinavians who had skied in their youth in Europe and was the first such organization in America and certainly the oldest continuously operating ski group in the country. It is very likely that the hills around Berlin, New Hampshire, were the first in all the land to be used for ski trails and it is the well-founded belief that this was the birthplace of Nordic skiing in America.

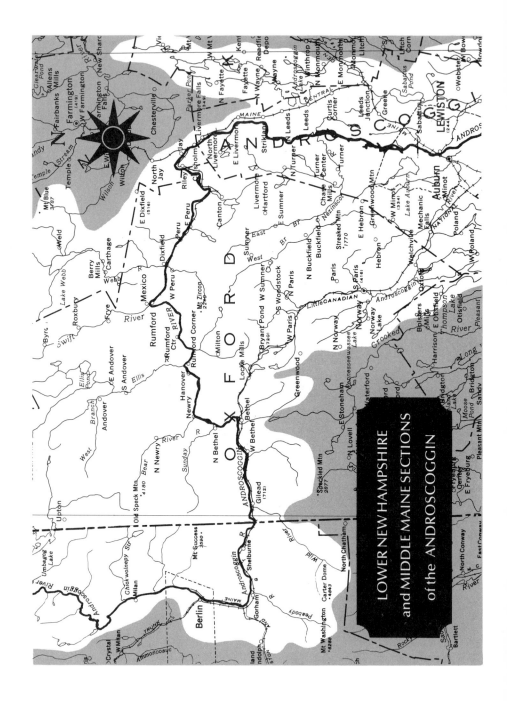

LOWER NEW HAMPSHIRE
and MIDDLE MAINE SECTIONS
of the ANDROSCOGGIN

38 / *Evolution of a Valley*

CHAPTER 7

Berlin Falls

to the

Maine boundary lines

The altitude of the riverbed has fallen some eighty feet from Pontook Dam to the city limits of Berlin and as the stream enters Berlin it has reached about 1100 feet above sea level. The river actually does enter Berlin, for this small industrial city of 16,000, give or take a few, is built on both sides of the stream and its biggest and almost only industry, the Brown Company, with its various mills and facilities straddles the upper part of the river-bisected town. Here, in a stretch of about two miles, was the real upper falls of the Androscoggin River. The falls were originally a series of cataracts with a drop in that distance of nearly three hundred feet and the white settlers took advantage of the water power possibilities for grain milling, sawmills and finally paper and pulp production.

The city proper is literally surrounded by mountains and is one of the most beautiful natural sites in all of New England, but man has combined with industry to take away much of its charm. First, the beautiful river bank is cluttered with ugly, industrial structures which completely hide the river, and much of the volume of water is diverted by dams into the mills for industrial purposes. Pulp and paper mills must have millions of gallons for their processes. This would not be so bad if it were not for the chemical wastes which were added to the river on its short passage through the mills. It is here that our wonderfully clear mountain water began its shameful pollution. From the Canadian border to Berlin some hundred and thirty miles of tributaries and river are pure, drinkable, and unpolluted, but below Berlin? "Well," as one conservationist once expressed it, "no self-respecting squaretail or salmon could live five minutes in it."

The second detraction from the charm of Berlin's natural location is also attributable to its industry. This is olfactory, and one must say that it is not as bad as it once was, due to a change in process of the company's pulp mills. However, until very recently, for the casual visitor who drove through and stopped for gas, the odor could have caused him to streak out of the filling station without waiting for his change or for the service attendant to put his tank cap back in place.

Citizens of the town debated both of these allegations by saying, "Economically there would be no town without the mills and furthermore, the mills are spending millions to combat the pollution, and as for the smell, well, you get used to it within a few hours, and too, it's rare that it is this bad because the prevailing winds are the other way." This last was the same argument, regardless of which part of town the speaker happened to be in at the moment.

The city of Berlin is roughly Y-shaped with the river running the length of the right arm and down the leg of the Y. The left arm of the Y runs westerly through a narrow valley which is cut by Dead River, a small stream which runs into the Androscoggin after crossing under Main Street in Berlin. At the bottom of the Y and at Berlin city limits and the Gorham town limits, is Cascade, the site of another Brown Company mill, and the settlement around it which is part of both Berlin and Gorham. Actually there is very little open space between Milan, Berlin, and Gorham, and in any other locality but New England a greater Berlin would have been formed which would include all three communities. New Englanders, with their Town Meetings, are acutely jealous of their boundaries and authority and nowhere else in America are there as many "twin cities" which are separated by either a bridge or sometimes just a street, as witness: Portland, South Portland, and Westbrook; then Lewiston and Auburn, then Bangor and Brewer; all in Maine. New Hampshire, Vermont, Massachusetts, Connecticut, and Rhode Island are also subject to this same "unto-getherness."

The river has been running generally south for all of its miles from its sources and certainly the valley itself has, up to this point. At Gorham the massive slope of the White Mountains begins and the river has to veer directly east for some twenty odd miles to Bethel, Maine. Gorham, the town proper, runs about two miles along the south bank of the Androscoggin and is a beautifully situated town which has not been esthetically marred by the industry in Berlin, upon which it depends economically. In fact, it is a typical, small, New England town with its full quota of white church spires and magnificent vistas of the towering Presidential Range on the south and the Mahoosuc Range on the north.

Gorham, like Milan but considerably larger, is in truth a suburb of Berlin and could be called even more rightfully a part of the city as probably ninety percent of the wage earning citizens are commuters to the mills and offices of the paper company in Berlin. The other ten percent provides services to the tourist trade, both summer and winter. Gorham is the gateway to the White Mountains from the north and east and therefore its motels and service stations are profitable enterprises all year-round. Many of the executives of Brown Company reside in Gorham or in the neighboring eastward village of Shelburne. Whether this is due to the less salubrious atmosphere of Berlin in times past, or to the American tendency to live in the country away from the office or plant, or whether the adjacency of ski resorts like Wildcat, Jackson, and North Conway just over the notch, is not known, but most Gorhamites would live nowhere else.

Just east of the village proper and across the Peabody River, which flows into the Androscoggin here but rises in Pinkham Notch at the crest of the White Mountains, is the town line between Gorham and Shelburne. Shelburne is a straggling town seven and a half miles in length, built along the intervale on both sides of the river and between the towering ranges which rise sharply on both sides. There are hardly four hundred residents in the town but again the largest proportion are dependent economically on Berlin industry, with a small number employed in resort inns and motels. The Shelburne Birches which line the highway on the south side of the river are world famous. The last of the Brown Company dams is located in Shelburne, this one being a low power and water control dam.

CHAPTER 8

Gilead
through
Canton Point

At the eastern end of Shelburne
is the Maine state line and the
river which started in Maine again becomes a "State of Mainer" but
from here to the mouth in Merrymeeting Bay she was never able to
recover her pure, sparkling, mountain stream qualities. She tried, but
just when she had begun to purify herself, by the addition of sweet
clean mountain water from her tributaries and the settlement of the
foul dregs dumped into her from above, she ran out of distance and
came to another industrial complex like Rumford and all that had been
gained was lost. In fact, there was a "build up" so that when her end
was reached in Merrymeeting Bay, she was a loathsome sewer which
no game fish would try to ascend.

Just after the river crosses the state line into Gilead, always accompanied on the south bank by the highway and the Grand Trunk
Railroad which joined the river at Berlin, Wild River comes tumbling

into the Androscoggin from the crest of Black Mountain. Here is added its pure spring-fed water to the putrefaction which had spoiled our big river in so short a distance.

Through the tiny village of Gilead and for about ten miles to the town of Bethel, the river flows through the characteristic intervale valley with islands now dotting the stream. At Bethel, however, the easterly flow suddenly points due north for about five miles during which it is joined by two more mountain streams, Sunday and Bear Rivers, and then at the hamlet of Newry it again points easterly. At Bethel it has lost its companions of many miles, U.S. Highway No. 2, and the Grand Trunk Railway which had taken the more direct southerly cant into Lewiston-Auburn by way of another tributary of the river, the Little Androscoggin, which the river meets at Auburn.

From Newry the river winds northeasterly past the villages of Hanover and Rumford Point where the Ellis River, another important tributary, joins it, adding pure water. It is a sad commentary on our civilization that as the river reaches Rumford (just above the town), tests showed that it had almost recovered, by self-purification, its pristine purity. It was still not quite drinkable, but far less contamination was present. In fact, black bass, about the most hardy of our game fish, were caught occasionally in the seventeen-mile stretch of water between Newry and Rumford. Below Rumford, alas, it is doubtful if even a rugged mud catfish could have survived.

The nature of the flow changes from Gilead to Rumford due to the very gradual drop in altitude of the river bed in this stretch. There are very few swirls and eddies or rapids, but rather a sedate and steady flow between intervale banks up to the beginning of Rumford Falls where the river is pinched between high hills on both sides and dashes first north and then makes a U-turn east and south around a point of highland and the island which contains the enormous Oxford Paper Company plants and the business section of Rumford. As one drives into Rumford on the highway which follows the river from Bethel the view on its northwest bank of the beginning of the falls is a spectacular one and fearsome in the wild abandon of the volume of water descending. It is easily seen why early settlers were fascinated by the latent power of the waterfall. The river drops in this U-turn about two-hundred feet and the power and paper companies have taken full advantage of this by the use of canals, flumes, and dams. In fact it is this network of canals which creates the island mentioned above, cutting across the neck of the land projection and through the powerhouses and mills and bypassing the U of the river.

The residential section of Rumford proper is mostly across the river on the west bank and running up the sides of the mountain. Directly opposite from the curve of the U, and dividing the town of Rumford from the town of Mexico, is the Swift River, (also the Maine Central Railroad which once ran to Bemis at the foot of Lake Mooselookmeguntic) another tributary which pours its volume of mountain fed water into the Androscoggin.

Here again we find the New England penchant for town independence for these towns are really one and the same community but retain their distinct governments. Rumford, with its close to ten thousand and Mexico with nearly five thousand inhabitants, but each with their own fire and police departments and town fathers, are again communities almost totally dependent on one industry. Here it is the Oxford Paper Company, an integrated pulp and paper concern which specializes in fine book papers and coated magazine paper for the "slicks." In fact, this was said to be the largest book paper mill in the world under one roof, and a tremendous roof it is.

Again, as in Berlin, there was not only water pollution, but also air pollution. Again the natives would give the same arguments anent the minor irritations of the latter and the company efforts to cure the former. Nevertheless, they were definite detractions to the river and the town.

After the river makes its U-turn and heads southeast again for about four miles from Rumford proper, it passes between the twin towns of Dixfield and West Peru. At Dixfield, on the north bank, the little Webb River joins the Androscoggin. This stream drains Webb Lake and its surrounding country some fifteen miles north of Dixfield. Dixfield village is, and always has been, a woodworking town, woodworking in all of its ramifications. Many woodsmen go into the forest and cut timber for pulp cordwood and hardwood for the industries of the region which manufacture clothespins, dowels, and other small items for the big Diamond Match factory across the river in West Peru. The remainder either work in the small woodworking plants or farm the intervales which line the river.

The elevation of the river at Dixfield is 416 feet above sea level and for the next nine miles to Canton Point, in which distance the river falls only twenty feet, it resumes its sedate way through intervale land on both sides. This is a beautiful canoe trip, with prosperous farms

As the river swings eastward into Maine, the last of
the Brown Company dams below Berlin frames a view
of New Hampshire's majestic Mt. Washington.

and pleasant rural scenes on either side of the river. The sense of virgin woodlands and primitive wilderness is gone, replaced now by pastoral vistas. At Canton Point, the river, which is heading almost due south again, does a U-turn and heads northward around the huge intervale which is the Point and which was the largest Indian plot under cultivation in New England and the headquarters of the Anasagunticook nation and their largest village.

About three miles after passing Canton Point the river flows almost due north again. Then it swings toward the south as the river bed is once more pinched between high hills on both sides at Riley where it again becomes a fast-water stream. Here there is a low dam which formerly served the dismantled International Paper ground-wood mill, but now provides tumbling water which is beneficial in restoring some oxygen by aeration.

A short distance below Riley at Jay on the south side of the river the International Paper Company completed in 1965 an enormous pulp and paper mill which stretches for nearly a mile along the bank of the river. This is a modern facility for the production of high-grade, bleached, kraft pulp and lightweight bond and specialty papers. River water here is diverted into the complex, and while the residue from processing was first treated in a primary clarifier, only some 25 to 30 percent of the oxygen destroying elements were removed during the first few years of operation. A secondary treatment plant eliminates some 90 to 95 percent of suspended solids from the processed liquids flowing into the river.

Below the dams at Jay, a growing village now that the new mill is there, and into the adjoining village of Chisholm (which is in the town of Jay and where the Otis Mill of International Paper is located), one enters, without noticing the difference, the town of Livermore Falls. This is another typical industrial river town whose population of about 4,000 has been markedly increased by the building of the industrial plant just above it. Livermore Falls ends the middle Androscoggin Valley which, for convenience sake, we call the stretch of river from the New Hampshire line to this point. Beyond here the geology and economy of the valley change considerably.

New Hampshire's Mahoosic Range (above) and Presidential Range (below) determine the Androscoggin's course in these two views from the Shelburne, New Hampshire area.

CHAPTER 9

the
Lower Valley
. . . Livermore Falls
to the sea

In following the river below the Rumford-Jay-Livermore area of fast water, we immediately enter a section of valley which differs from the geology of that above in that the valley widens considerably between much lower hills. For about thirty miles there is a much more gradual drop in altitude above sea level than in any like stretch above, being only about thirty feet of differential for the distance. Here there is evidence of a lake which was dammed in prehistoric times at Lewiston Falls and must have covered some four hundred square miles, including most of the present towns of Livermore (east of the River), Turner, Wayne, Monmouth, Fayette, Leeds, and Green, as well as the west portions of Winthrop, Readfield, and Mt. Vernon. It was also no doubt dotted with islands, but the contour of the present is indicative of a very large lake which, when the river cut through at Lewiston, was only partially drained. Much of the territory still has

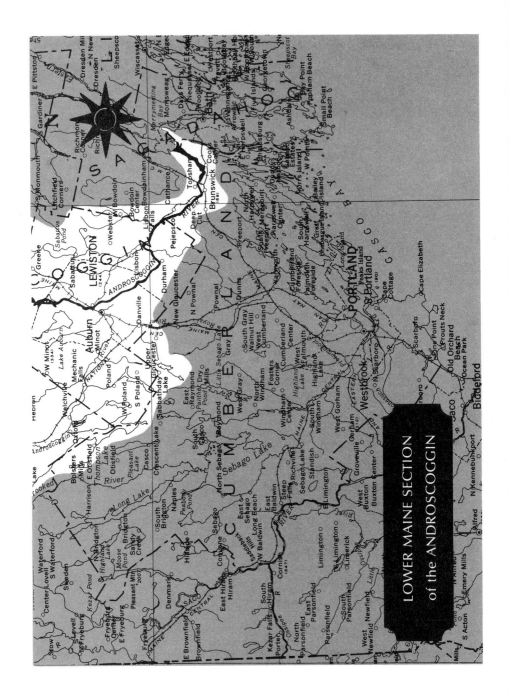

LOWER MAINE SECTION
of the ANDROSCOGGIN

lakes and swampy bogland, so the stream seems rather sluggish in this stretch.

Two tributaries of the river enter in this section: the Dead River, which drains a chain of ponds, starting with Parker Pond in Mt. Vernon, Crotchet Pond in Fayette, Lovejoy Pond at North Wayne, and Pocasset Lake and Androscoggin Lake in Leeds. The Dead comes into the river from the east and the other one, the Nezinscot, enters from Turner on the west. About two miles below the mouth of the Nezinscot the river widens out into Gulf Island Pond, the man-made lake created by the Gulf Island power dam seven miles downriver. The lake, while only a quarter of a mile to a mile in width, is a perfect example of the restraining faculty of polluted water. While it did serve as a settling basin for a small amount of the chemical waste matter from above, it was until very recently offensive enough to have precluded the development of the shores for residential use in what would be the most attractive sections for suburban homes in Lewiston on the east bank and Auburn on the west bank. Alas, these developments moved away from the river, justifiably so, to avoid the stench of the abused waters which at times was abominable.

The eastern boundary line of Auburn, which is the western boundary line of Lewiston, runs down the middle of the river. The northern boundaries of both towns cross the lake just above Gulf Island Dam so that the river flows between the twin cities for the next dozen miles.

Lewiston Falls, another of the characteristic series of cataracts, has two comparatively low dams in the five miles of rapids. The first, at Deer Rips, is the supplemental dam to the high Gulf Island Dam. The second one, of great granite blocks, is really a combination of several separate dams which divert the river into the canal complex which parallels the main business section of Lewiston and which noticeably cuts the volume of flow over the falls and the spectacle of the cascades. Here again, in Lewiston on the east bank, industry along the river has erected a conglomeration of factory buildings which hang from the banks like dissolute old women draped over a railing. These in Lewiston, however, are textile mills, and along most of the river proper are woolen mills, the old four and five story variety, some brick and some frame which cause sleepless nights for the Lewiston fire chief.

The canal, which is diverted from the river at the dam, runs southeast and is tunnelled under bridged Main Street to service the rows of enormous textile mills (cotton and synthetics) which were for many years the economic backbone of the city's life. In very recent years, however, the industry of the area has become more diversified as electronics plants have come in replacing some of the lost textile operations which have fled either south or into oblivion. Shoe manufacturing has largely replaced space left in the old textile mill buildings.

Lewiston, however, is still an important fabric manufacturing center, the largest of the remaining textile mills, The Bates Manufacturing Co. (Lewiston Division), being in full operation as are newer plants in other production lines.

The population of Lewiston, the second largest city in Maine, is about forty-five thousand of which roughly seventy percent is of French-Canadian ancestry. Auburn, just across the bridges, of which there are two in the main business sections of the cities, is a shoe manufacturing town of some twenty-five thousand. Here, although there are some French, the majority are of Anglo-Saxon descent. The waterfront of Auburn is not quite as cluttered with disreputable old mill buildings since the shoe industry, not requiring the volume of water needed by the textile mills, has largely grown up several blocks away from the river, on the railroad and recently on the western outskirts. Urban renewal has greatly improved the river frontages.

A short distance downstream from the business sections of the two cities are the several outlets from the main canal which flow through the textile plants and accumulate more chemical waste and dyestuffs to add to the already effluvial mess which our river had become.

On the Auburn side of the river, and in almost the center of population of the town, another tributary, the Little Androscoggin, flows into the big river. Unfortunately this one differs from most of those above, for the story of the Little Androscoggin is very similar to that of the big one in that it has been pretty well contaminated by industrial waste and raw sewage dumped into its comparatively short length of less than fifty miles. It too rises in mountainous country from spring sources and its entire length is dotted with little industrial towns among which are Bryant Pond, West Paris, South Paris, Norway, and Mechanic Falls.

In these towns are located a paper mill, shoe factories, tanneries, and textile mills, as well as many small woodworking plants, and much of their refuse found its way into the Little Androscoggin. Therefore this tributary did not contribute to the purity of the waters which finally enter Merrymeeting Bay. True, in the towns of Oxford and Mechanic Falls there join the Little Androscoggin several outlet streams which drain an area of some hundred square miles of what has been relatively pure and uncontaminated water. This did assist in the repurifying process of the Little Androscoggin River just prior to its junction with the big river at Auburn. These streams are the outlets for the several ponds and lakes in what is known as the Poland Spring area. Thompson Pond, the largest, whose outlet is in the village of Oxford, and the outlets for Tripp Pond, Green, Hogan, and Whitney Ponds, come in at the hamlet of Welchville (in the town of Oxford) and are joined at Mechanic Falls by Range Brook which is the outlet for Upper, Middle and Lower Range Ponds. These adjoin the grounds of famous old Poland Spring which for many years was known universally for its tremendous tourist hotels and the world-wide distribution of its Poland Spring water.

The Poland Spring House, the largest of the buildings at the resort, was taken over by one of the "Great Society" agencies for the training of underprivileged girls in 1966, and at the Town meeting of 1967 in Mechanic Falls, there arose a terrific argument against a proposal by the operators of the school for diverting their sewage, which had grown to alarming quantities, into Middle Range Pond, after treatment. The furor, of course, was caused by the fact that Range Brook is the drinking water supply for the town of Mechanic Falls.

The process of contamination continued, since some thirteen miles below the mouth of the Little Androscoggin the Sabattus River flows in from the east and adds its pollution. That short stream, less than twelve miles in length, has waste contributed by the towns of Sabattus, Lisbon, and Lisbon Center.

Several miles below the Sabattus mouth is the next series of rapids at Lisbon Falls. U. S. Gypsum has a plant here for the manufacture of insulation and formerly the big Worumbo Woolen Mill, (later the Lisbon Weaving Company) also added waste to the river.

Three miles below Lisbon Falls at Pejepscot, the bottom of Lisbon Falls Rapids, again a diversion dam canal flows through a paper mill. This time the Pejepscot Paper Company contributes its waste, though not pulping waste, simply "white water" or the waste drainage from the paper machines.

Four miles downriver the Androscoggin greets the historic old town of Brunswick, the oldest continuous habitation on the river. Here it swings north and east around the point on which the city is built and flows northeast its remaining six miles until it empties into Merrymeeting Bay.

At Brunswick and its adjoining town, Topsham, across the river, are two control and diversion dams which serviced a small paper mill on the east and the Cabot Textile Mill on the west (now discontinued and converted to a discount shopping center) but the waterfront is not as cluttered with ungainly industrial buildings as the others upstream. Brunswick is not strictly a mill town, but the site of historic old Bowdoin College, and since World War II a big service installation, the Brunswick Naval Air Station.

After flowing by the congested area of Brunswick proper the river, winds around several islands, Cow, Driscol, and Cornish, and points northeastward into the gradual widening of Merrymeeting Bay. This bay is fed from the northeast by the Kennebec River and is really a bay of tidal water. The average rise and fall of the tide is almost ten feet. Even this is not the joining of the Androscoggin River with the sea, for the merged waters of the Androscoggin and the Kennebec, seeking the sea, flow through a narrow outlet at ebb tide into a seventeen-mile tidal strait which is miscalled the Kennebec River. This outlet is between two points, West Chops Point and Chops Point. The strait is the boundary, not only of the towns of Bath and Woolwich, but the waters of the respective rivers, Androscoggin and Kennebec. On the west side of the strait and the south side of the tidal Bay (Merrymeeting) is the city of Bath.

Bath is a typical New England town of ten thousand, totally dependent upon its shipbuilding industry, but unlike most of its fellows, it has maintained comparative economic well-being through peace, war, depression, and boom. This is largely due to the Bath Iron Works and its satellite industries, the Hyde Windlass Company and others which furnish components for naval vessels. The Iron Works has been building naval vessels for generations, from Civil War gun boats to the latest in electronic marvels in destroyers and submarine killers, and recently commercial vessels and tankers.

A dozen miles below Bath the joint waters of the Kennebec and the Androscoggin flow into the Atlantic and diffuse their contaminated waters into its healing depths.

3

the Developing Valley

CHAPTER 10

Brunswick

. . . settlement through

the 19th century

Of all the towns on the Androscoggin, Brunswick's early his-
tory records the most starts and stops, settlements, then destruction
and abandonment, all followed by new settlements and destruction,
for, as told earlier, it was the only river site in the valley where the
Anasagunticooks were actually faced by English settlers. It was not
until after the departure of the Indians that the settlement on the
Pejepscot Falls of the river became permanent. By 1793, the town was
incorporated though the transactions of transfer of ownership had
been many from much earlier times, with the Purchase, Wharton, and
finally the Bagley-Little grants and sales and the complications involved in the titles of the various claimants. After the Bagley-Little
grant was made the movement of families into the area was promoted
and Topsham, just across the river, became the focal point of gradual
migration upriver where the villages of Lisbon and Lisbon Falls on the

right bank, and Durham on the left, were to become small rural centers. The two towns, Topsham and Brunswick, are again examples of local town independence and are separated by the narrowest part of the lower river and connected by a bridge from one main street to another, which is somewhat like Lewiston and Auburn. There are certain differences, however. Topsham has always been more a town of homes and less a business center than Brunswick, and with the exception of a few neighborhood grocery stores, most Topshamites shop in Brunswick's business section.

Historically, however, the two towns were united by events which were indistinguishable from one another. Even the economic and disaster records of the two are quite uniform, with Brunswick always maintaining a two to one, later three to one, majority in population. The record of industrial efforts runs parallel, with the establishment of little grist and sawmills on both sides of the river, beginning quite early in the eighteenth century. The pattern of disasters to these efforts was more attributable to the river than to destruction by fire, as was true of the mills upriver. The geology of the town locations here, at the sudden narrowing of the river gorge as the stream makes a U turn, created not only a water power potential, but also made every sudden rise in water level a menace to anything on either bank. While the situation was very similar to that in Rumford, with Brunswick built on a promontory creating the upside-down U bend, the retaining higher ground on both sides of the lower river was not sufficiently above sea level to contain very much rise in volume. From as far back as 1723 there are listed what the writers of the time chose to call "freshets." Accounts of staggering losses to the communities of bridges, dams, and mills with all equipment "carried away by this year's freshet" were many. The river above Brunswick, between Pejepscot Falls and the narrows at Topsham is quite wide and comparatively slow as it spreads out over low banks in a wide basin. This part of the river freezes in a normal winter, with ice covering the surface to a depth sometimes of three or more feet. In the spring when the ice goes out this mass of gigantic ice cakes jams up as the river narrows at Brunswick, and when it does break through often creates a flash flood situation of great ice hunks sometimes weighing tons and projected with dynamic force through the narrow aperture between the two towns. Anything in the way of obstructions, such as bridges, dams, and buildings erected too close to the river banks, is carried away in a swirling rush to Merrymeeting Bay. Dredging operations in the bay have turned up a mass of miscellaneous objects, some as heavy as 100 H.P. boilers of heavy iron plate, which, over the years, were swept away by "freshets" of flooding and ice jams.

In 1835 an engineer, one Leammi Baldwin of Boston, surveyed the river above and below Brunswick and issued a paper called "Water Power in Maine" in which he said that the geodetic lay of the land and river at that point was equal to any in the eastern United States in power potential and prophesied that it would become a great industrial center. That his prophesy did not come true was due to several things but mainly due to the fact that the early promoters of industry in the two towns were not of the caliber or the ability of the small group of men in the Lewiston cabal who did foresee and plan and carry out their dreams. They were for the most part local men of limited financial resources, and did not secure expert hydraulic engineering advice based on a broad plan for full use of the river's power as did the Lewiston pioneers. So they, and most of them were strictly interested in sawmill operations, went their way alone, building wooden dams at various parts of the area for limited use of water through flumes and short diversion baffles to turn their saws and grindstones. The mills were mostly profitable for short periods, or until floods or fire swept them away whereupon they were rebuilt and the cycle started all over again. That it was profitable was due to the availability of overseas shipping facilities. These operators did not have to forward finished products such as boards and shingles some hundred miles on expensive transit routes as did the lumber people further upriver. Also they thought the supply of logs which came down the river from above was inexhaustible, but they were in error on this score.

In the early nineteenth century, Bath, only a few miles from Brunswick and Topsham, had already become a ship building center of note and was a ready market for much lumber. Most of the lumber could, with care, be rafted from the mill to the shipyards. Brunswick was not only a sawmill center rivaling Bangor and Stillwater on the Penobscot, but during this period was an important contributor to the technology of the whole New England lumber industry. In 1820 the circular saw was invented and the firm of Eastman and Jaquith of Brunswick received the patent and began producing the tools in their foundry and machine shop there. It was the first big breakthrough in speeding up the processing of logs, for before that time all sawing had been done by the old up and down method of waterpowered rigid saw blades which was slow and costly. Later the band saw was introduced and proved a further improvement, but it was too late to help the Brunswick mills, for it was after the Civil War.

Ship building had also crept around the "Chops," the outlet of Merrymeeting Bay and up both shores of the Androscoggin and on the islands that dot the stretch: Freyee, Mustard, Driscoll, and Cow, even though these islands were apt to be swept over with each spring freshet. The market was there at the mill owners' doorstep, and the spring drive of logs each year always provided ample raw logs which were not stopped at Berlin or Lewiston but landed in the Brunswick booms. These booms were the successors of the early ones used for the purpose of stopping and storing the King's Masts in pre-Revolutionary times, and in fact, after that war in 1789 when it was not necessary to save the beautiful long sticks of virgin pine for the Royal Navy, logs left in the King's pool below the falls were used to build the new booms, mostly above the falls.

The boom company which was incorporated as the Androscoggin Boom was chartered by the General Court of Massachusetts with the right to hold all logs which came down the river for the logging interests and to charge a fee for each log released. By 1820 the company had eleven booms, six above the falls and five below, and some of these booms lasted seventy-five years, others less than that. The freshet of 1855 carried out three booms with all of their logs with a loss of $40,000, though whether the Boom Company or loggers sustained the loss, is not clear. The booms were constructed of logs driven into the river-bottom and forming piers which were filled with stones. These were connected by long timbers fastened with irons and chains which made a surface barrier across the river, sometimes backing logs up for miles while awaiting their use by the mills below.

All of the above events certainly indicate that the towns of Brunswick and Topsham were lively and busy communities during the first half of the nineteenth century and rightfully so. The beginning of the century also provided the entire Maine area with its first seat of higher education and an institution which was to have far reaching effects not only on the area but the country as a whole. In 1794 the General Court at Boston passed a bill establishing Bowdoin College. The site of the college was to be in doubt for some time as there was pressure from no less than six different groups to have the new institution located at Gorham, Portland, North Yarmouth, New Gloucester, Freeport, and Winthrop, all in Maine. As a compromise, Brunswick was selected. The name was chosen because James Bowdoin, a distinguished Bostonian, gave money and land valued at $6,800 for its establishment. However, the sum was not sufficient to begin building and it took some eight years for the promoters to raise enough additional funds. It was not until 1802 that the doors were opened to eight students and the college graduated seven recipients of degrees in 1806. The same commencement conferred fourteen honorary degrees on prominent men who (it is recorded) requested the honor and later were to be benefactors of the institution. It is noteworthy that one of these men was Everett Saltonstall of Boston, the great-great grandfather of the long-time Senator from Massachusetts.

The list of graduates and degree recipients during the next hundred and fifty years was to contain many names among the most distinguished in the country in letters and public service. The Class of 1825 started the long procession of notables with Henry W. Longfellow and Nathaniel Hawthorne and continued with such luminaries as President Franklin Pierce and Vice President (under Lincoln) Hannibal Hamlin, as well as Admiral Robert E. Peary and Commander MacMillan and many other leaders in state and national scenes. The faculty has had outstanding men such as Longfellow, who taught modern languages there for several years before going to Harvard, and Joshua Chamberlain who graduated from Bowdoin in 1852, then taught religion at the college until 1862 when he accepted a leave of absence to become one of the most distinguished soldiers in the Union Army as commander of the famous Maine 20th and later a major general. He returned to Bowdoin in the fall of 1865 and resumed his professorship, but only for a short time as he was elected governor of Maine and served from 1867 to 1871.

Visitors to the Bowdoin campus today are all advised to see the stately Bowdoin Pines after they have explored the beautiful old buildings, the splendid libraries and the remarkable art collection, which incidentally contains paintings of Rubens, Van Dyck and Titian, as well as portraits of Thomas Jefferson and James Madison by Gilbert Stuart. The grove of trees at the edge of the campus is well worth seeing and remembering. These are virgin white pines with enormous girth and rear up over a hundred feet and stand as a perpetual monument to what was the forest covering of the whole Androscoggin Valley in the days when Champlain first saw Merrymeeting Bay. They are the only ones left in the valley and to the best of this writer's knowledge, in the whole of New England.

At first the business people of the town did not accept the college with the pride which developed later, and there was a definite rift in opinion between "town and gown" in many matters of public interest such as the growing feeling for abolition of slavery which was becoming an issue in the fifties. The college was a hotbed of anti-slavery sentiment, due to the religious influence of its largely clerical faculty and the business people who were quite the opposite since their enterprises were so dependent upon shipping and lumber and whose owners were strongly opposed to anything which might upset the status quo of trade with Southern ports, lumber exports and cotton return cargoes. However, these men were unable to stem the rising tide of abolition sentiment and certainly had no idea that a book written on one of their own quiet streets was to be the catalyst for the war to come. For that matter it is doubtful if Harriet Beecher Stowe had any such idea either, though her brother, Henry Ward Beecher might have been that hopeful.

At any event, when war did come to the two towns, Brunswick, with about 4,700 population and Topsham with 1,700, contributed as heavily to the war effort as any similar towns in New England. Nearly seven hundred men went into the armed services from the towns (plus Harpswell which comprised most of the peninsulas and islands below Brunswick) and included the "Fighting Parson," Josh Chamberlain, who alone made the contribution notable.

There was considerable loss of manpower in killed and wounded and "died of disease" and in prison, but the loss of shipbuilding due to the ironclads which came out of the war was much more serious to the economy of the towns. This began an erosion of the sawmill and shipbuilding business which gradually, by 1900, had changed Brunswick from a bustling shipbuilding center and one of the largest lumber exporting ports in the country, to a quiet college town with its cultural accomplishments its greatest pride.

There had been one rather ineffectual effort to make Brunswick a textile center which its promoters felt would rival Lowell and Lawrence, Massachusetts, one day. In 1834, shortly after Baldwin's *Water Power in Maine* was published, local interests organized the Brunswick Company and built an enormous spinning mill structure on the Brunswick side of the falls. It was of stone masonry 146 feet long and 45 feet wide, towering five stories above the river. It had a capacity of 5,120 spindles and ran for six years before inadequate financing and possibly poor management caused it to fail. It was leased to another operator in 1840 who ran the company only three years before failing and it then was sold at auction to Boston interests who also subsequently failed. In 1847 it was operated by a concern called the Warumbo Manufacturing Company (not to be confused with the big Worumbo Woolen Mill which operated at Lisbon Falls for many successful years) which also went into receivership in 1853. It is interesting to note that the operators of the company had rather peculiar rules for the practices of hiring and firing of employees. One of these read in the instructions to foremen, "No person shall be hired or retained who habitually absents themselves from public worship on the Sabbath, or who uses profane or indecent language in the mill or elsewhere, or who uses ardent spirits as a beverage." Whether these rules had anything to do with the failure of the management to make a success of the enterprise is not positively known. At any rate, the mill was finally sold in 1857 to a company which apparently knew what it was doing, the Cabot Manufacturing Company. A Boston concern, it was well financed and expanded the operation and successfully operated as many as 35,000 spindles until the 1940's when the textile business in New England was at its lowest ebb. Then the Cabot Company closed, sold the machinery to South American interests, and left Brunswick. The great roomy buildings which now covered many acres of ground, were converted to a big discount center with abundant space available for small industries.

CHAPTER 11

the

Twin Cities'

early settlement

and the

beginning of industry

The settlement around the Falls at what is now Lewiston was started some years later than the little colonies which had sprung up all along the coast after the departure of the Indians. Brunswick and the east coast of Casco Bay had been sporadically settled much earlier. While the Falls had been visited by hunters and traders, the first settler in the Lewiston area came in 1770. He was a Massachusetts colony man named Paul Hildreth, a name which has come down to this day among prominent Maine citizens. Hildreth was sent to Maine by Jonathan Bagley and Captain Moses Little, wealthy Boston merchants who had obtained a grant in 1767 of five square miles of land on the west side of the river around the Falls. Hildreth built a cabin near the present site of the former Continental Mills textile plant and was followed shortly by two others, Pettingill and Varnon in 1771. Lawrence Harris came about the same time. It was the summer of 1770 or

1771 and he was accompanied by eight workmen who helped in the erection of the framework for a gristmill at the Falls. They went home for the winter, returning in the spring to finish the mill and finally settling in the new plantation. Harris was the first to use the river for power at this point. He received large grants of land from Bagley and Little for his services and in turn brought settlers in.

During the seventies and throughout the Revolution the little community grew slowly and by 1788 there were seventy-six families in the township. Incidentally, it was noted in early records that only three soldiers in the area served in the Continental Army, though by 1793 when the town had grown to over three hundred families, there were said to be some eighty-odd veterans of the Revolution among the breadwinners. This was true all through Maine as veterans much preferred land script in the virgin territory rather than to accept worthless Continental currency.

The town was chartered in 1795 and combined with the plantation of Gore. There has been found to this day no reason for the name Lewiston Falls, though the most accepted theory is that the name was used for some reason by a member of the Massachusetts General Court, rather than the unpronounceable Indian name, Amitgonpotook Falls, which the petitioners had attached to their charter application.

Across the river in what is now Auburn, as well as on the Lewiston side, Colonel Moses Little (who was Captain Little in 1770) of Boston, was agent for large tracts of land. In 1797 the first settler in that area was Joseph Welch, followed soon by others among whom was one Boblemyer who built the first gristmill on the Auburn side of the river, though on the Little Androscoggin near the present New Auburn section. It is interesting to note here that the descendants of Colonel Little, who was the original grantee, were to become the most influential citizens of the twin towns and their progeny have long been prominent in Maine and are to this day. This was apparently the case both in Lewiston and Auburn where family names have had a degree of continuity, although this was not true of the other Androscoggin Valley towns.

Among the names of early settlers in Lewiston were Ames, Herrick, Wright, Barker, Bearce, Coburn, Coffin, Littlefield, and Garcelon. A descendant of the last named was to be the first Democratic governor of Maine and the others are still prominent names in politics and business in the state. In Auburn, in addition to the Littles, there were the Smalls, Moodys, Starbirds, Baileys, Emersons, Caswells, Briggs, Merrills, Reeds, Webbers, and Jordans. Both towns were strictly agricultural, with small grist and sawmills as the only touch of industry, and those only for local needs. Both communities grew and in 1809 Moses Little erected a large grist, carding, and fulling mill driven by waterwheel near the falls on the Lewiston side. The mill burned in 1814, which was a long existence for the times, since most mills had a life of only two to three seasons before being gutted by fire.

When the War of 1812 broke out it had an immediate effect on the region, contrary to the mild reaction of the upriver communities. This was no doubt due to the close proximity to the coast and the older communities as well as better communication between Boston and Maine ports, such as Portland, only thirty miles removed. At any rate, a company of militia was organized under Captain Oliver Herrick and saw action with heavy casualties at the Battle of Lake Champlain. Later two other companies formed a regiment under Colonel Blaisdell and fought until the end of the war.

The period of 1818 to 1830 saw a number of sawmills erected and burned, according to schedule, but the towns were becoming lumber centers with logs being driven down from the woodlands above and manpower trickling in from the booming lumber business at Bangor and the other Penobscot towns of Stillwater and Old Town. Up to this time the prospects for the future prosperity of the area seemed pointed at lumber, and the power potentials of the great falls had apparently not been considered for textiles. However, there were a few forward-looking citizens who had other ideas, and in 1834 a group of Lewiston and Auburn men interested some Boston capital in the organization of the Lewiston Falls Manufacturing Company, capitalized at $100,000, an immense sum for the times and the place. They built a mill below the falls for the manufacture of satinet, which Webster describes as "an inferior grade of satin containing cotton." This was the first textile mill in the area to be operated continuously for over forty years, though it was partially washed away by the freshet of 1837 and later rebuilt.

While the great development of the falls for textiles was to await certain events during the next fifteen years, the increase in sawmill activity continued unabated. Mills were built on both sides of the river by Samuel Bearce, the Coe and Pingree interests of Bangor, and others. Drives of millions of feet of logs were coming down the river from as far upstream as the Rangeley Lakes where the first drive took place in 1837. However, the dream of a great textile center had been forming in the minds of some very astute Auburn and Lewiston citizens and in 1836 they formed a company with the unwieldy corporate name of The Great Androscoggin Falls Mill, Dam, Lock and Canal Company. The incorporators of this concern were mainly descendants of our old friend Colonel Moses Little, and were Edward Little, Josiah Little of Newberry, Massachusetts, Thomas B. Little, Josiah Little of Minot (Auburn), Samuel Pickard and another Edward Little, Edward T. They apparently did not do much in the way of announcing their intentions but quietly hired an engineer, B. F. Perham of Boston, to make an extensive survey of the falls and the water power possibilities. Perham was evidently one of the best in his field of hydro-engineering since the data which he produced was later used in the erection of the dams and canals which are still in operation in the 1970's and as efficient after a hundred years of constant use, as when built. The tentative layout of canals and the figures showing potential flowage are so nearly exact as compared to the present situation as to be uncanny and his original drawings are still safely stored in the vault of the Union Water Power Company in Lewiston, Maine.

During the next nine years the Littles and their associates made progress with the plans but most of their efforts and a great deal of their available capital was expended in acquiring land and water rights on both sides of the river at the Falls and clearing the titles. In 1845 the name of the corporation was changed to the much simpler and more easily remembered one of The Lewiston Water Power Company and a good deal of outside and much needed capital was brought in from Lewiston and Boston sources. The new company was launched and immediately plans began for construction of the Canal System and preparation for the construction of the dam which was to be of granite, and as one writer of the times described it, "of adamantine strength." Actual work on the canals was started in 1850 and was finished as far as 1100 feet on the upper or main canal in 1851.

Meantime a wooden dam had been erected and water began to flow through the canal. The delay in building the permanent stone dam was actually caused by the financial difficulties which the company was beginning to feel. Not only was the cost of the canals running much higher than contemplated, but the company directors were also very much involved in the completion of their grand plan. The plan included building a row of tremendous textile mills down the length of the upper and lower canals to absorb the power potentials of the diversion of water from the river into the canals, with flowage regulated at the canal head. The plan was to utilize this water in as many mill installations as could be built along a quarter-mile of land on each of the canals, upper and lower. The same water could be used over and over again as it sought its own level at the canal discharge points downriver from the falls, with about fifty feet of fall.

Between 1830 and 1850 there had been a steady population increase in towns of the lower valley. This was also true of the Little Androscoggin where the villages of Mechanic Falls, Norway and the Paris trio, South, West, and Paris Hill had all assumed the typical economic conformation of the area with marketing centers for the agricultural countryside and small manufacturing plants for the townsmen's employment. A small rag paper mill was built at Norway, little woolen mills at several of the towns, and saw and gristmills at all of them. Norway and South Paris (the town of Paris included both villages), with just over a thousand inhabitants each, were thriving communities which were to remain about the same size for several generations. Lewiston and Auburn had grown by leaps and bounds and by 1850 were almost the same size with about five thousand residents each. At this time they were predominately of English extraction, and mostly from roots in Massachusetts and sired by Revolutionary veterans just prior to the turn of the century. Now with the beginning of the canal construction and the building of the big mills, the Irish began to pour in. Many who came up with the railroad crews as the Atlantic and St. Lawrence Railway approached Danville (Auburn) Junction, deserted to go over to the stationary construction jobs where the wages were slightly higher for pick and shovel work and less backbreaking than rail laying, or so the recruiters for the Mill and Canal construction bosses told them. Thus was created in Lewiston, in the twenty years between 1850 and 1870, its first minority group to be considered quite inferior by the old Yankee stock, though it would have been difficult to convince an Irishman of any bit of inferiority.

The Boston Irish invaded at about the same time, and the integration process in Lewiston took about the same number of years, though it culminated in the accomplishments of Irish congressmen, senators and governors and Federal Court Judges only, not Presidents of the United States. There was, in the same period, another invasion of the town by still another ethnic group. The managers of the waterpower and textile developments were no neophytes at their trades. They were Boston, Lowell, and Providence business men who knew the weaving and spinning business and were in close touch with the labor markets of those places which were already humming with productivity. They were in position, as soon as the mills in Lewiston were ready, to divert certain skilled personnel from those textile centers to the lusty infant industry in Maine. We will not ask what glowing pictures they painted, nor what inducements they gave, for the industry then was not unionized and the life of even the most skilled weaver, spinner or "mule" tender was an economic gamble and the prospectus of the new mills in Maine carried such descriptions as "Company housing accommodations in sturdy brick buildings with all sanitary requirements." At any rate they secured the labor of skilled textile workers, and they built a row of "sturdy brick buildings" to house these key employees, along the north bank of the upper canal, facing the new Bates Mill which was to rise five stories in majestic grandeur above the canal. (The row has disappeared now and is mostly parking space for the merchants along Lisbon Street and the customers of several large supermarkets and the state liquor store.)

The textile workers were largely Scots and Englishmen. Their descendants had come from the crowded old world textile centers of Manchester, Leeds, and Edinborough to Massachusetts and Rhode Island, bringing their weaving and spinning skills in exchange for the vaunted freedom and opportunity of the new world. Their reasons for moving to Maine were much the same as their fathers' reasons for leaving Europe to seek the better life and opportunity of newer civilizations. These early textile workers in Lewiston were rapidly accepted by the natives for two reasons: they were of common English extraction, and also were of the same class of skilled artisans and hard working farmers who largely composed the early settlers. In addition they were Protestants, mostly of Presbyterian and Church of England backgrounds, and they naturally gravitated to the Protestant Churches which had flourished in both towns for a number of years. The Irish, on the other hand, were Catholic and anti-English and were for the most part either single or married men who would send for their families when they could. They were rough, uneducated, brawling, hard drinkers who would labor with pick and shovel in the canals all day and "drink and fight all night." But they were there to stay and stay they did as the segregated minority until the French-Canadians began to pour in twenty years later.

By 1860 the characteristics of the two towns had begun to crystallize, with Auburn assuming its role of a quiet churchgoing market town, a trifle disdainful of its brawling, fast growing, bustling neighbor. There were a few small industries, mostly shoe shops, springing up along the railroad which ran through the town a few blocks from the river, and one textile mill which had been built on the Little Androscoggin. It was not a manufacturing town until the shoe business reached its peak early in the twentieth century, and even then it maintained its rather superior attitude toward Lewiston. Some of this "air" was derived from the fact that many of the biggest business men of Lewiston chose to build elaborate homes on Goff Hill in Auburn rather than bring up their families in the rough industrial atmosphere across the river. Also Auburn had much the better schools including the Lewiston Falls Academy which had been established in 1835. This later became the Edward Little High School. Another observation on the variance of the two towns is political. Lewiston has been solidly Democratic in all elections for a good many years while Auburn has been a Republican stronghold. In our references to Auburn we use only that name to avoid confusion, for Auburn was known by a good many different names until it was incorporated in 1842 as "Auburn." Several of the names have since become sections of the town: Goff's Corner, Danville, Minot, and Poland (which in 1798 included the whole area). As a matter of fact the post office in Auburn was "Lewiston Falls" and was not changed to Auburn until 1854, twelve years after the town itself was officially named.

Unlike Rumford, Maine, and Berlin, New Hampshire, the two other industrial centers upriver whose developments were "one man" affairs, Lewiston and Auburn could not look up to a Brown or a Chisholm as the father of its great industrial development. Rather it was the group of men who first formed the Great Androscoggin Falls Mill, Dam, Lock, and Canal Company and hired the engineer. In short, the Littles and their associates who had the dream and their successors, a larger group, carried on the projects. In researching the efforts of these men one is struck by the fact that the directors and stockholders of all the companies who were instrumental in what was a remarkable industrial development for the times, were so interlocking that it was impossible to tell one company from another if looking only at the directors' names.

This followed through several generations, and in ownership and operation of the dams and canals included the Lewiston Water Power Co. and its successor, the Franklin Company. Its successor in turn, The Union Water Power Company, is the present operator of the dams and canals, and the stock is owned entirely by the Central Maine Power Company whose directors are as interlocking as were those of the predecessor companies. This common ownership and management went further in early days.

The boards of the first big mills to use the power of the river dams and canals were likewise composed of the same gentry as those of the water power concerns. The Bates Mill, which was the first of the big ones built on the main canal, had the names of Benjamin Bates, Amos Lockwood of Providence, Rhode Island, Alexander DeWitt, Thomas B. Little, Thomas I. Hill, Seth Fowler, and George Ward. All except Little and Lockwood were from Boston, and all were large stockholders of the power company and of the Hill Mill organized later that year. All were also involved in the Franklin Company which was organized in 1845 with a capital of $1,000,000. The purpose of this organization was to take over the financing and construction of the new textile plants, and if necessary to help in financing the cost of the dams and waterways. In fact, in 1857 it did just this by acquiring the stock of the Lewiston Water Power Company though the ownership of both concerns was almost identical.

The Franklin Company was to be an influential factor in the lives of both Lewiston and Auburn for over a hundred years and in the 1970's is still one of the important property owners in Lewiston and one of its largest tax payers. The Franklin Company did not remain an owner of Water Power through this long period, however. The name of the Water Power Company was changed again to its present form, The Union Water Power Company. Franklin maintained ownership until 1901 when the individual mill corporations bought its stock.

With the introduction of additional capital from the Franklin Company, the grand plan went forward with the completion of the cross canals and the lower canal, extending the canal to 1900 feet in length by 1851 and to 4200 feet by 1865. Meantime the wooden dam was partially washed out in the freshet of 1862, and work was started at last on the granite dam of "adamantine" strength using temporary wooden coffer dams to keep up the flow in the canals. The great dam was finished in 1865 and the figures on the canals shown by water company records are: upper, 4,200 feet long with 28 foot head; lower, 1,600 feet long with 22 foot head. The canals were generally 60 feet wide.

In 1856 the Maine Legislature chartered the Maine State Seminary and after some bickering as to the site of the new academy, it was decided to locate the school in Lewiston. In 1864 the name was changed to Bates College and collegiate courses were added. This was made possible by a gift of $100,000 from Benjamin Bates who also promised an additional $100,000 if other friends of the school would match this sum. By 1867 this was done and that July the college graduated its first class of eight degree recipients.

As in most New England institutions religion played a vital part in the origin of Bates College. Oren B. Cheney, a Dartmouth graduate and a Freewill Baptist Minister, conceived the idea of converting Maine State Seminary into a liberal arts college and it was he who secured a college charter from the State of Maine in 1864 and obtained financial support from Benjamin Bates.

Cheney served as the college's first president and led the young institution through its first crucial years, a period of growth in buildings, funds, and academic recognition. This expansion continued from 1894 under his successor, George Colby Chase, until 1920 when Dr. Clifton D. Gray became the third president.

Over the years the college had become more non-sectarian and under its fourth president, Charles Franklin Phillips (1944-66), made probably its most definite advances in physical equipment and endowment while following his predecessors' concept of a small New England liberal arts college with excellent facilities and moderate tuition costs. The fifth president, Thomas Hedley Reynolds, was inaugurated in 1967.

The Bates College campus is one of the most attractive in New England being situated on a hundred acre plot in the Lewiston residential area. There were nearly forty buildings of attractive traditional architecture, ample for the use of the 1,200 students, 73 percent of whom are from New England, 23 percent from states outside of New England and 4 percent from foreign countries.

The population figures on Lewiston during the period of 1850 to 1880 give a very fair idea of the prolific growth in the industry of the town: 1850—4,584; 1860—7,424; 1870—13,600; 1880—19,083. The jump between 1860 and 1870, when the population nearly doubled, was of course caused by the Civil War and the boom in textiles which followed. It was apparent that cotton somehow had made its way from the Confederate States to Maine because there were few shutdowns for lack of raw material during the war.

Why the Lewiston mills appeared to fare better in their supply of raw material than other New England mills is not quite clear. The reason may never be known. It certainly had to do with the procurement of a great deal of cotton which was technically illegal and though both the federal and confederate governments condoned the practice of trade between their enemies when it was thought to be advantageous, still it was certainly hush-hush business. Apparently few if any records were kept of the thousands of bales of cotton which came from Mississippi, Alabama, Tennessee, and other points in the blockaded South. It is known that much of it came North by rail from Memphis to St. Louis, Louisville and Cincinnati and then by way of several routes to the East. Much of Lewiston's share came by way of the Grand Trunk Railway System, but whether it came from the southern terminus at Portland or from the Canadian section is not clear. Probably both routes were used in addition to the direct steamer connection to Portland from all shipping ports.

It is quite apparent that Benjamin Bates in Boston acted as purchasing agent for the Lewiston mills, certainly including the Bates, Androscoggin and Hill, and he was quite successful. From scanty correspondence between Bates and the local mill managers which remains in files of The Union Water Power Company, it is evident that somehow foreign and American cotton came through to Lewiston. There is mention of "Surat," "Pernambuco" and "China" cotton as well as American, and a quote from a letter of April 9, 1863, from Bates in Boston to Lockwood in Lewiston is revealing: "We received 23 bales of American Cotton from the west and has come forward through Mass. Also 99 bales shipped from New York yesterday by steamer to Portland. This cotton came through Mexico and the bales are small."

And on September 3, "American is up again. We cannot buy cotton to-day and make fine goods and get cost—. We took in connection with the Pepperell Mills to-day 75 bales of very low American and 200 bales of raw gin cotton—. The report is that there are but 13,000 bales of Cotton in New York including Surat."

It is generally conceded that a great deal of the cotton which came into New England from the enemy Southland originated or was handled in New Orleans by the controversial Ben Butler. Actual records of General Butler and his brother, Andrew Jackson Butler, are indeed scarce, particularly after Butler left New Orleans, though the black market operations continued through brother Andy who was said to have piled up a fortune of several millions in strictly "legitimate" trade.

Transportation, or rather the lack of it, was the apparent reason for the ten year delay in the development of the power potential of the falls after the Littles' first dream of an industrial complex there. The river was not navigable, as we know, and when Perham's figures were completed the Littles knew that they would have to bring in an amount of capital which was far beyond their resources. However, they did attempt to interest the big textile people centered in Boston, and no doubt were told that when rail transportation was assured for an outlet to markets they would come into the enterprise. This was done, when in the forties Josiah Little of Portland promoted the Atlantic and St. Lawrence Railway and construction started towards Danville Junction. You will note that the name Josiah Little was one of the same names appearing in the original incorporators of the Great Androscoggin Falls, Mill, Dam, Lock and Canal Company, but which one he was is not clear. There were two Josiahs, one from Newberry, Massachusetts, and one from Minot, Maine, which was to become Auburn. It is presumed that it was the former, though the records of the railway indicate he was from Portland. However, he was of the same family and descended from Moses Little and was a cousin of the Minot Josiah. He was certainly an ambitious and farseeing pioneer who realized the tremendous possibilities of the falls at both Berlin, New Hampshire, and Lewiston, and knew that rail transportation was the missing link which must be supplied before his dreams could be realized. It is strange that he overlooked the great falls at Rumford and bypassed that chance when the rail line followed the Little Androscoggin past West Paris, rather than skirting the falls at Rumford. However, it is possible that to include that route was simply beyond the financial resources of the new rail line.

The rails reached Auburn and were extended by a short line known as the Lewiston and Auburn Railroad Company from Danville Junction to Lewiston. This was operated as a shuttle to connect with the Atlantic and St. Lawrence and was leased to the Grand Trunk when the Atlantic and St. Lawrence was built. It is assumed that the promoters of this little railroad were the same shrewd entrepreneurs who engineered the mills, canals, dams, and everything else anent the grand plan. The two towns, through bond issues, raised $300,000 to build the spur line, retaining common stock for the communities in proportion to the bond subscription, $225,000 for Lewiston and $75,000 for Auburn. The road was leased to the Grand Trunk in 1873 for 99 years and in 1972 the lease was renewed with some changes.

Prior to the building of the railroad, communication with the coast

Two of the Union Water Power Company dams which
harness the seasonal variations of the Androscoggin's
flow; the Errol Dam just below the junction of the
Magalloway (top) and the Lakes Dam at Middle Dam,
Maine.

and the older communities below had been confined to a fairly improved road from Auburn to Portland and another from Auburn down the river to Brunswick. Traffic over these roads from the middle thirties was quite heavy, with teams of loaded goods pulling great wagons in summer and horse and ox powered sleds in winter. There was also regular stage service several times a week on both routes. The advent of the rail line eliminated the Portland freight and passenger hauling, but the stage lines to Brunswick still covered the eighteen miles in about four hours. To quote an advertisement in the *Lewiston Journal* of July, 1855; "A pleasant journey along the beautiful Androscoggin in luxurious coaches, leaving the station in Auburn at 8 o'clock and arriving for lunch in Brunswick at noon, Fare $1.25." It is interesting to note that the fare from Auburn to Portland, some thirty miles on the railroad with a scheduled time of one hour, was the same, $1.25.

Through the middle decades of the century and almost up to the time of the coming of the rail line to Lewiston Falls, there had been a strong conviction among loggers that Lewiston would one day be a lumber center as important as the Bangor area. With this thought in mind a number of Penobscot lumber people had invested in vast timberlands around the lakes at the headwaters of the Androscoggin and had made some investments in sawmill property at Lewiston Falls. Among these were Coe and Pingree of Bangor who had also gained control of water rights at Errol, New Hampshire, by a New Hampshire charter as the Androscoggin River Improvement Company, later the Errol Dam Company, and by a Maine charter as the Richardson Lake Dam Company for the control of water rights at Upper, Middle and Lower Dams, on the Rangeley Lakes. These charters set up in each case a schedule of charges for logs spilled through the dams which varied from 3c to 6c per log driven over the dams' spillways.

The owners of these companies were all Penobscot men, Jacob Hazen, L. E. Dunn, and E. S. Coe, with the Pingrees as silent partners. They felt by this control and a substantial interest in the sawing at Lewiston, that they could maintain a virtual monopoly on wood products in the whole valley. However, they did not figure on the astuteness of Josiah S. Little and his associates in the Winslow Company at Berlin, New Hampshire. That company's location and its ability to process the total production of logs in the upper reaches of the river, made control of just the dams a costly and lawsuit-ridden proposition which defeated their purpose and actually turned Lewiston from lumbering to textiles. The Lewiston and Auburn woodworking area gradually assumed the minor role of processing only the timber of the surrounding countryside, not the great volume cut in the upper reaches of the river. Several of the lawsuits mentioned were of great interest at the time and one, the case of *Coe* v *Errol* which hinged on "goods in interstate commerce" being taxable was finally decided in the Supreme Court of the United States in favor of Coe et al, and set up a law precedent which has been used ever since in cases involving individual states', cities', or towns' ability to collect taxes on goods in transit through these political subdivisions. What happened was that Coe et al, were caught by low water at Errol dam in New Hampshire, and had to hold several million feet of logs at the dam. The wood blocked river traffic for a year, therefore the town of Errol and/or the County of Coos, New Hampshire, assessed heavy taxes on the logs for that period. The New Hampshire courts held for the town, but the Supreme Court reversed it and set the long held precedent.

While the sawmill industry in Lewiston went out of business, the owners of the dams on the upper river simply continued to charge toll on logs and later on pulpwood which were sluiced over their spillways each spring and went to the Winslow Company (later Berlin Mills) at Berlin. There was always a question as to whether these charges could be justified since the charters had originally put a time restriction on charging tolls and limited it to first, the recovery by the dam company of the cost of the dam, then to simply the cost of upkeep of the dam. Rather than go into costly litigation it is apparent that the lumber, and later the paper companies, continued to pay some tolls on all wood driven. This was satisfactory to both the dam owners and the lumber and paper interests, though both are apparently reluctant to admit it. Now, however, all driving is finished so there is no reason for secrecy any longer.

Despite the manpower shortages which were caused all over New England by the Civil War, the population of Lewiston jumped in the seven years between 1863 and 1870 from 8,761 to 13,602 and it was evident that the rapidly expanding textile mills were the reason. In Auburn, however, during the same period there was no noticeable increase in population; it remained about 6,000. The shoe business had boomed during the War but the big expansion in Auburn's shoe shops did not take place until 1870. Also it is recorded that Auburn's proportionate number of Union Army men was much higher than

Lewiston's, being nearly 500 volunteers and draftees, or 10 percent of her population.

Lewiston's contribution, on the other hand was about 700 or about 7 percent of her population. In justice to Lewiston, however, which had many more veterans afterwards, there were families which had moved to Lewiston during the war but had sent sons to the Army from their former home towns so that they were not counted in Lewiston's quota. More manpower was lost when young men did not return to their home towns after the war. Maine and New Hampshire were in the midst of the third wave of a westward moving migration, principally men who were following the previous exodus of loggers and woodsmen to Michigan, Minnesota, and on west. Despite these losses Lewiston continued to draw new citizens, for the mills were expanding and calling for more workers. Generally speaking these new textile workers were older men and women and still of the same English-Scotch ancestry.

In the 1870 directory of Lewiston and Auburn published by W. F. Stanwood only some thirty names which seem to be of French origin are listed in both towns. Of these, seventeen are Garcelons, and while they were originally of French ancestry they were not emigrés from French Canada but were descendants of Reverend Peter Garcelon, a French Catholic priest who renounced Catholicism and fled to the Isle of Guernsey where he became minister of the Church of England and married an Englishwoman. One of their sons, James, emigrated to America and was one of Lewiston's first settlers (mentioned previously) and in 1870 Dr. Alonzo Garcelon, a grandson of James Garcelon, had just returned from his services as a surgeon in Grant's Army and was elected Lewiston's first Democratic Mayor in 1871 and Governor of Maine in 1878. Nothing is known of the other thirteen French names, but it is probable that they were the vanguard of the wave of nearly six thousand French Canadians from lower Quebec Province who swarmed into Lewiston during the ten years before 1880 when the town's population reached twenty thousand. By 1872 the good ex-Canadian Frenchmen had erected several Catholic Churches and the Irish were delighted that the somewhat unwelcome "Frogs" no longer attended mass at St. Joseph's which had been in existence since 1850. Later, by consolidation, the enormous Church of Saints Peter and Paul was to be formed from the French churches and would become one of the largest parishes in New England. Parochial schools were soon opened and for many years, in fact until World War II, classes were taught in French with English offered as a foreign tongue.

It is probable that nowhere in America had a foreign segment of a community's population retained through several generations such close conformity to its customs and particularly language, as the Lewiston French had,* actually until the 1940's. By this time they had become nearly 70 percent of the City of Lewiston's approximate population of 40,000. Here was as nearly a segregated society as was possible, yet it was of their own doing. It was not that the old families of Yankee stock did not feel slightly superior, because they did when thinking of the average Frenchman, nor that there was not some social intermingling, for there was. The upper five or ten percent of the French who had achieved economic advancement in commerce or the professions, particularly politics, medicine, or the law, were accepted in most strata of municipal society in Lewiston and even Auburn, but it was a thin segment. There was intermarriage, but the vast percentage of the French population lived together in certain sections of Lewiston, worked together in the mills, worshipped together in the Church of Saints Peter and Paul and spoke together in "Canuck" or Quebec French, an argot which a Parisian Frenchman would find very hard to follow. Until comparatively recent days it was impossible for a person to get a job as a clerk in a Lewiston store unless he or she was bilingual, which meant "Do you speak French?" which really meant do you speak "Canuck." This situation continued until after World War II when the several thousand lads came back to Lewiston after their rough years' service in the Army and Navy of the United States where they had been subjected to an unholy amount of ragging from fellow GI's about their accent. For most of the second and third generation of Lewiston Frenchmen, while they did speak English (as a second tongue), spoke it with an accent as thick as bouillabaisse and all were called either "Frenchy" or "Frog." To their credit, they came home pretty well Americanized and insisted that English be spoken, where none had been through three generations. Too, at about this time, the Catholic head of the parochial school system was successful in securing a change of curriculum which demanded that all classes be taught "in English." The result is remarkable in the quality of the language which is spoken. When shopping in Lewiston stores at the present time or walking down Lisbon Street or riding a bus, you are

*A possible exception is the Mexican-Spanish area in the southwestern United States.

seldom out of hearing of French, but if you look blankly at your questioner he or she will immediately grin and ask the question again in almost accentless (except for the Yankee twang) English.

The reason for the French invasion was simple; the mills were expanding and the old Scotch-English weavers and spinners were becoming foremen or were leaving the mills for outside work or retirement. There were no sources for textile laborers now in Massachusetts and where there were such workers they were going up to nearby mills in Manchester and Nashua, New Hampshire. The Maine mills were beginning to be very cost conscious and wages were lower than Massachusetts or Rhode Island. True, living expenses were supposed to be lower, but the old Anglo-Saxon classes were getting used to a higher scale of living and someone had to man the looms. There had been a trickling of French woodsmen coming down to take the places of the westward moving Yankees and many of these men had gone to Lewiston at the end of the drive. They were family men, not single buckaroos like their predecessors, and here in the States were jobs not only for Papa, but for Mama and fourteen-year old Pierre and Marie. Consequently they went back to their barren little farms in St. Etoile, packed up their belongings, sold their horses and set out for "Lewis-Tone." There they settled, camping out a few weeks with Cousin Armand who had brought his family down earlier and now had five of his boys and girls working in the "Androscog" Mill, and then getting a "rent" of their own and becoming citizens of Lewiston.

Meantime the Irish had been absorbed into the society of the two towns, mostly Lewiston, however, and Irish lawyers and contractors were the coming leaders in business and politics. Lewiston itself was soon to be the sole hotbed of the Democratic party in Maine. The Irish influence was originally the strongest but it was gradually taken over by the French, as they became the segregated majority, rather than the minority.

The little band of stockholders of the Franklin Company and the textile mills, whose basic property was the flowage rights of the river, had accomplished much of their grand plan by the middle of the seventies. They were not satisfied, however, with their lack of control of the headwater lakes, for as long as outsiders controlled the level of Umbagog, Richardson, and the big Lake Mooselookmeguntic, the operation of the mills on the canals in Lewiston was dependent not only on the vagaries of weather and freshets, but on the control of the dams at Upper, Middle, Rangeley, and Errol by the Bangor owned dam companies which could lower or raise the water flow at will. While there were certain other legal responsibilities pertaining to the "public good," they were only interested in collecting tolls on logs which now generally went on to Berlin, New Hampshire.

The men in Lewiston had long wanted these properties as they were dependent upon a fairly uniform flowage for the canals to furnish power to the textile mills. The original owners of the dam companies had mostly passed from the picture and stock in these companies was largely held by trustees for the Coe and Pingree heirs who were interested only in getting a good price for the properties. They were not interested in further development on the Androscoggin.

In view of these facts, in 1877 negotiations were begun which culminated in the Franklin Company acquiring the four dams and water rights for a total cost of $365,000. This enormous sum for those times was composed of $165,000 of Franklin Company money and $200,000 furnished by the City of Lewiston. The latter was raised by the city's $200,000 bond issue. Proceeds were turned over to the Franklin Company in return for a contract between the city and the company, their heirs and assigns, whereby power would be furnished to the city without cost for the operation of their pumping station for domestic water, fire protection and other purposes. This involved 600 HP which was raised to 750 HP in 1887 and continues to this day with no obligation of the city as to maintenance of the system.

The entire transaction involved a multiplicity of negotiations and at the time was considered a coup by the little group of promoters in the Franklin Company group, with all of the advantages gained by them, but in the long run, nearly a century, it is apparent that the city did not come out on the short end. Actually in terms of water power and taxes imposed on the water company, the $200,000 advanced has long since been exceeded in benefits to the city. The matter of city taxes on The Union Water Power Company's water rights is still in dispute from year to year but no compromise is yet in sight.

Regardless of the actual long-term advantages gained by the parties, there is no possible doubt but that the deal at the time it was concluded involved an extraordinary amount of shrewd political manipulations in the sale of the plan and the subsequent ratification by the voters. Meantime, The Union Water Power Company had become the successor to the Lewiston Water Power Company then the Franklin Company, and while it changed ownership several times during the following ninety odd years, it controlled the water level and flow of the entire river for all of that time. The Franklin Company held its stock until 1901 when it sold the ownership to the individual cotton mills which were dependent upon the water system for their operating power.

During the ten years between the Lewiston-Franklin Company deal on the dams and 1887, there were beginning to be complaints about the city's domestic water and in that year the city obtained permission from the state legislature to pump water for its domestic needs from Lake Auburn across the Androscoggin River. While the complaints had largely been because of discoloration and off-taste qualities, nevertheless, during the same period all over the United States, there was much agitation and fear of typhoid infection from the river waters, though no epidemic occurred in either Lewiston or Auburn. It was decided to use the water from Lake Auburn, a wise move for the excellence of both cities' water supplies has been an asset for generations, and the industrial and municipal pollution which followed from 1890 on would possibly have been catastrophic.

Across the river in Auburn the shoe manufacturing business was becoming important to the economy of the region. Existing shoe shops were expanding. The sewing machine, which had been invented in 1846, was being adapted to shoe making and what had been largely a handicraft industry was becoming mechanized. Auburn, with a nucleus of skilled shoemakers, was a natural point for development. The existing factories began to expand, building additions to their shops and installing the new machines, so that by the beginning of the nineties such firms as John F. Cobb and Company, Ara Cushman Company, Wise and Cooper, Dingley-Foss and Smith, Pray & Company were humming with activity. It is interesting to note that the terrific increase in population of Lewiston in the twenty years between 1850 and 1870 had very little effect on Auburn's very slow, but steady growth. However, beginning soon after the Civil War Auburn had its industrial spurt with shoe manufacturing and its population doubled to 11,250 between 1870 and 1890. Still it maintained its atmosphere of a quiet orderly churchgoing New England town. Youngsters (or adults) who were interested in kicking up their heels did not do so in Auburn, but went across the bridge to the more flamboyant fleshpots of Lewiston. The shoe business, however, with its ups and downs through the years, was to be Auburn's economic barometer for nearly a century, until the 1960's when the town began to attract important new industries.

CHAPTER 12

the

Middle Valley

in the

nineteenth century

The settlement of this portion of the Androscoggin watershed differed slightly from the upper valley in that most of the settlers came into the Maine territory during and immediately after the Revolution and consequently pre-dated the New Hampshire towns by some twenty years. Also, as noted later in the story of the upper valley, the towns of Bethel, Livermore, Paris, and Gilead (Peabody Patent) actually served as a source of the settlement of the New Hampshire towns of Shelburne, Gorham, and Berlin.

The river towns of Gilead, Bethel, Rumford, and Livermore were started through grants made originally from the British Crown, but in most cases to absentee proprietors, and later confirmed by grants from the General Court of Massachusetts to the original grantees or their heirs. None of this land was settled permanently until many years after the original grants had been made. The terms of almost all grants were that the proprietors should colonize the land, either by themselves or, as usually was the case, by organizing colonies and selling the land to others. The price of land set by the proprietors after the Revolution was nominal and in many cases practically free. The proprietors knew that the land retained would increase greatly in value upon development by the colonists. It followed that a vast number of continental soldiers who were dissatisfied with the conditions in their homes when they returned after the war, readily accepted the offer of cheap or free lands in the territory of Maine. Between 1788 and 1800 they swarmed into what was to become Oxford County, Maine, and the intervales of the Androscoggin and the Little Androscoggin drew many of these pioneers. Here was cheap but fertile land which required very little clearing except for the homesites, which usually were built on the hillsides overlooking the rivers. A town in New England bears a slightly different connotation from that in other parts of the country, and here does not necessarily mean a collection of inhabitants in close proximity but rather a section of countryside which may, and usually does, contain several villages, but still subject to town laws set forth by town meetings of all qualified voters and administered by selectmen elected by the voting populace of the entire town. These elementary rules hold until the legislature sees fit to incorporate a city as such, when a city charter is adopted and officials elected to legislate and administer city ordinances and rules.

The early history of Livermore was typical of the settlement of most of the towns on the middle section of the Androscoggin, with the exception of Rumford. In 1773, Lieutenant Elijah Livermore, with two companions, came to survey the town for the original proprietors. They came up from Boston by boat to Hallowell on the Kennebec River and set forth overland for the location by way of Winthrop, crossed Androscoggin Lake in borrowed canoes, then paddled down the Dead River to the Androscoggin and up that stream to approximately the location of the village of Livermore. Here they laid out the boundaries of the town. According to rumor, the Deacon, as he was called later, took very long strides in pacing off the boundaries and ever after the town was somewhat larger than the original grant. The party, camping on the river bank, spent the summer in marking off lots in the town which did not at that time bear the name of the Deacon. They returned to Massachusetts in the fall with charts for the proprietors to use in the colonization plans, but times were so unsettled that actual colonization did not begin until ten years later when Deacon Livermore himself moved his family and others into the new country. In 1789 there were seventeen families living in the town and farming the land. In 1795 the General Court of Massachusetts incorporated the town as Livermore, which was proper, as the Deacon had been father and promoter to the settlement and had, so it was said, very shrewdly amassed a fortune in the sale of land for the proprietors and increased the value of his own holdings. In 1810 the population of the town was 1,560 and it was a flourishing farm community with several gristmills and a few general stores, churches, and school houses. Communication with Danville (Auburn) and the coast had been opened by passable roads and already the old-timers were complaining of the exodus of young men from the town as soon as they reached maturity. It is true that this was happening in all of the towns of the middle valley. The war with England which broke out in 1812 was excuse enough for many to get away from farm life to the adventure of soldiering, then later to migrate up the Penobscot and Kennebec to go "loggin' " and later still, up their own Androscoggin to the big woods of the North Country. The abandonment of farms, however, did not begin until much later, but in a time of tremendous families the population managed to stay about the same until the eighties when Livermore had gone from about 2,200 down to 863 in the census of 1880.

Up at the New Hampshire line there were two very early grants, Peabody Patent (present day Gilead) which is a mere hamlet, and a very early grant made at the end of the Indian Wars to residents of Sudbury, Massachusetts, for military services against the red men. This was called Sudbury-Canada and it remained simply a grant in name only until 1768 when it was confirmed after much wrangling to the heirs of the original Indian War veterans and a township was affirmed to Josiah Richardson and his associates. Eight years later, in 1776, one Ingalls, the first permanent settler, came to the wilderness and was followed by others so that in 1781, at the time of Tomhegan's raid (mentioned later) there were ten families settled in the intervales. It was from among these people that some of the captives were taken by Tomhegan to Canada and the raid also caused so much panic that some left for the coast and never returned. However, a garrison of militia was established on the river at the place and new settlers came in so that by 1796, the fear of Indians having been removed, there were nearly one hundred families in the town and the Massachusetts General Court incorporated the town as Bethel. Despite the continuing passage of many of the settlers to the upper valley, the town grew and prospered due to a combination of farm economy and small mill enterprises similar to those in Shelburne and Gorham above. By 1810 the population had grown to nearly a thousand souls and ten years later thirteen hundred, but like the other towns of the valley, by 1880 it had shrunk to half that figure.

Gilead was incorporated in 1804 and the pattern of population change was similar, with 215 in 1810, 328 in 1820 and a dreadful fall off to only 88 total population in 1880. Most of the decrease in population could be attributed to the industrial development of Berlin and this is confirmed by the names on the town rolls during the early part of the century which appeared later in Gorham and Berlin. The move to the towns for cash wages began in the area very early, and abandoned farms were plentiful in this part of the valley.

Bethel was more advanced in its cultural and spiritual development and in 1799 it brought to its newly organized Congregational Church a man who was to dominate the life of the town for many years. This was the Reverend Daniel Gould, who hated the devil and all his works and whose salary to start was very high for the day, being $180.00 per year plus $150.00 additional in labor, one-third of the salary to be paid in cash and two-thirds in produce. The good Reverend accepted the stipend, provided a "few cords of fire wood" were also furnished. Bethel Academy was formed in 1836 to provide higher education for the boys and girls of the town. This became Gould Academy in 1842 because of a small inheritance left by Daniel Gould to the school, provided the name be changed. The school has had a long and distinguished history, providing high school education for the town of Bethel and preparatory school facilities for boarding students from far and near. Its scholastic standing is comparable with better known private schools.

It is interesting to note that in the Civil War the little town of Bethel, with only some 1,500 inhabitants, sent 195 of her sons to the Federal service in contrast to the disinterest in the war in industrial Berlin, just 25 miles upriver.

In the early days of the nineteenth century, despite the activities of such zealots for purity as the Reverend Gould and his peers in the other valley towns, rum and other spirits were considered a necessity in all well-regulated homes and the taverns did yeoman service in supplying the wares, both in drink and "take out" form. An extract from the account book in 1796 of Twitchell's Tavern in Bethel shows an interesting price list of wet and other goods: "1 gal. Rum $1.33; 1 pt.

Rum .18c; ½ gal. Molasses .40c; 1 lb. tobacco .26c; 1 lb. sugar .17c." Fifteen years later prices had apparently gone up as "1 bushel Potatoes cost $1.04; ½ mug Toddy was .14c but 1 night's lodging was only .14c." Inflation had not really set in at that time.

As previously described, there are roughly forty miles of river between Bethel and Livermore in the middle valley, and about half-way between the two rural towns is Rumford and its satellite towns of Mexico and Dixfield. Hence it might be thought that the development of these towns would be parallel. The difference was due to the industrial development of the waterpower potential of the cascades and falls at Rumford. This, however, came much later than in Berlin upriver, though the rapidity of the growth development, when it did come, was much more evident.

The town was formed originally by a grant of the Massachusetts colony in 1774 to replace the original proprietors of Pennycook, New Hampshire, whose original grant had been reassigned to others by the General Court of New Hampshire when that body had been separated from the Massachusetts Bay Colony. The wrangling of the dispossessed proprietors forced the General Court to replace in the wilderness of the Maine territory a tract somewhat larger than the one at Pennycook. Since this land was plentiful, the General Court felt very fortunate at getting rid of the troublemakers. Thus Pennycook in New Hampshire, which later became Rumford, and still later, Concord, the capital city of the state, was left to its Hampshire men grantees and the old proprietors accepted seven square miles of land on the "Ammenoscoggin" River at the "upper falls." However, it was the upper falls as far as they knew at that time, or at least it was the upper falls in the territory of Maine. The grant was reapproved by the Commonwealth in 1779 to the proprietors, who as usual never occupied the land themselves but attempted to settle it by colonization in the usual manner of sales and grants to coastal dissidents and revolutionary veterans. It was extremely slow work, however, and by 1781 there were only three families in the area and they fled to New Gloucester near the coast when the renegade Indian Tomhegan made his raid on the towns above in August of that year.

The slowness of the settlement was no doubt partially due to the report of the surveyor, one Samuel Titcomb of Wells, who laid out the lots for sale to the new colonists, and reported that the terrain was rocky and not much fit for agriculture except at certain intervals above and below the townsite and on the Swift River which comes in at the present town of Mexico. In fact the only good things he had to report were covered by his statement, "The Ammoscogin River abounds in Salmon and Shads and has good mill sites."

Despite the unattractiveness of the plantation there were some more or less permanent settlers in what was then called New Pennycook. Some of their difficulties were set forth in a petition to the Massachusetts General Court not long before the "plantation" was incorporated as the "Town of Rumford," excerpts from which are as follows:

"To the Honourable Senate and House of Representatives of this Commonwealth etc: — this petition of the subscribers of a plantation called New Pennycook in the county of York or Cumberland [there seemed to be some doubt as to their location] humbly showeth: That whereas your honours have seen fit to lay a tax on said plantation of ten pounds and add, we, as a plantation met to consult upon same, but we found ourselves so few in number (only 22 families and 8 single men, which absconded in winter season.) Therefore we found ourselves unable to pay said tax."

The petition then continued to list the difficulties of the plantation:

"Being 70 miles from Portland, the nearest market, the roughness of the roads, all supplies, including salt must be hauled on horseback in summer and on foot in winter through dreadful snows . . . our inability to advance one shilling for a day's preaching or schooling for our children".

There is no record of any reply from the General Court but it is assumed that the Commonwealth was unable to collect its ten pounds of taxes due.

However, despite these conditions the town did grow with farms scattered up and downriver on each side of the falls and by 1810 there were 629 men, women and children occupying the town. By 1830 it had reached its greater population of 1,894 which was to shrink, like the other towns, to a mere 844 by 1880, but its rejuvenation was underway by that time and here it differed from Livermore and Bethel.

The real reason for the growth in the first thirty years of the century, however, was the first use of the falls for industry and the tributary streams for small mill sites. Most of these were combination grist and sawmills with the familiar overshot water wheels. Daniel Gould described one which was operated during 1820-23 by Rufus Virgin and Nathan Knapp as "a carding and a shingle machine, a sawmill and a gristmill carrying two pairs of stones, by the same water." He also went further in his description of the area around the falls to say that in 1826 there were no bridges over the river but the villagers were served by three ferries above and below the falls. The forest nearby provided the raw materials for the woodworking plants and particularly the vast stretch of country reaching northwest toward the Rangeley Lakes and up the tributaries of the Androscoggin: the Bear, the Ellis, and the Swift Rivers. Driving logs down these streams was a far simpler matter than via the main river in New Hampshire.

The Reverend Gould had left his church in Bethel to answer a call to the congregation in Rumford as he felt that the devil was challenging more vigorously there. He still maintained his interest and love for Bethel which had been his first ministry and a particular concern for the education of the children of his old pastorate. In 1826 he wrote out in long hand, "A history of Rumford from its first beginnings to the present times" and while it was never published, it was read and saved in his papers in the form of a much dog-eared manuscript. In his description of the spiritual life of the town he made the following amusing statement, "There is only one man in the town who has had a full public education, viz; Rev. Daniel Gould. He has been in this town and Bethel 28 years, in the work of the gospel ministry." Curiously, the other most prominent man in the little town was its only lawyer, Peter Virgin, who had been educated at Phillips-Exeter and Harvard and whom the Reverend does not mention in his entire treatise, though he, himself, had not received any education beyond that of a small academy in Massachusetts. There must have been some coolness between the pulpit and the legal profession.

The town, despite the Reverend Gould, appears to have had its full quota of roistering rum-bibbers and there was always, during the first half of the century, a plethora of taverns and even general stores which handled all of the available spirits. The cheapest was a concoction known as New England Rum or potato whiskey, which must have been rather fiery stuff; next and somewhat higher in price was West Indian Rum and for a few cognoscenti there was imported brandy and wine. All homes kept a supply of spirits and it was said that even the Reverend Gould was not averse to taking a social glass in his parishoners' homes, though he was "death" on drunkenness and profanity. In Maine there were stirrings against the demon rum by the early temperance societies which, while getting a foothold in 1829 at Bethel, Livermore, and Dixfield, created no interest in Rumford until

1850. Meantime, the first state liquor license law in the United States was passed by the Maine Legislature in 1821 just one year after the state was created from the Commonwealth of Massachusetts. While it was said that the law was not enforced very well, the state did remain the pioneer in liquor legislation by passing a law in 1846 limiting the sale of spirits to "medicinal and industrial" purposes. In 1851 Maine became the first dry state in the Union by prohibiting the manufacture and sale of intoxicating liquors. This became a part of the state constitution in 1884 and remained on the books until the repeal of 1934. Thus Maine became not only a pioneer in temperance legislation, but also the pioneer in liquor scofflaws, and the town of Rumford appeared to be the leader in this respect in the middle valley. In fact, enforcement of the law throughout its life was a dismal failure and though the Pine Tree State was *technically* dry for eighty-three years, it was said that there was never a time in all of those years that it was not possible to find "spirits" in most of the towns of any size and certainly the Androscoggin River towns of Rumford, Lewiston, Brunswick and Bath. Perhaps the approvers of the eighteenth amendment and the Volstead Act of 1918 might have hesitated in their overriding of Woodrow Wilson's veto of the act if they had been more familiar with the failure of Maine and the other dry states to legislate effectively against the drinking habits of Americans.

While the population of Rumford had been decreasing slowly since the 1830's and had dwindled to about 1,400 from its peak of 1900, the year 1850 began a very much faster exodus from the town, and it was the building of the Atlantic and St. Lawrence Railway which was the cause. Josiah Little and his fellow railway promoters had decided to bring the rails up the more densely populated valley of the Little Androscoggin River through the thriving villages of Norway, Paris, and West Paris, bypassing the sleepy rural middle valley and joining the main river just before it entered the State of New Hampshire. The first rush of the exodus was composed of young ablebodied lads who wanted to work on the rail construction gangs. This was followed by growing trickles of whole families moving to the "railroad towns," for they were going to be cities and would have big mills and business would boom, and "what could you expect from a river which was too filled with rapids and falls to ever amount to anything in the way of a means of transportation except for logs in the spring."

The Civil War contributed to the deterioration of the town, too, as it took about a hundred and fifty of the young men and very few of these returned to their home town, not because of battle casualties, but because they decided to settle elsewhere, usually in one of the railroad towns.

CHAPTER 13

settlement

of the

New Hampshire Valley

The geology of the New Hampshire-contained valley of the river made it even more isolated from the rest of the world than the lower valley and because of this its settlement was even slower. This was due to the fact that settlers had to come upriver from Maine because of the formidable mass of the White Mountains which blocked migration from the earlier settled regions of Massachusetts and lower New Hampshire. However, there had been some movement of pioneers up the Connecticut River but no drifting eastward toward the Androscoggin.

Passageway over the mountains from the Androscoggin Valley was frequently made by Indians on trails which followed the Peabody River up to the crest of what later was called Pinkham Notch, then down the Ellis River to the Saco River and the plains below, and another trail up to the crest of what is now called Crawford Notch, and then down the Saco River. However, white men were not known to have passed the barriers of the Presidential Range until 1771 when Timothy Nash and Benjamin Sawyer of Bartlett in the Saco Valley, chasing a moose, discovered the pass which later became Crawford Notch. The discovery of Pinkham Notch was made about the same time though not by Daniel Pinkham for whom it is named, for he did not come to Jackson until nearly twenty years later and not until 1824 did he build the road through the Notch to Jefferson.

However, first mention of the valley was probably made in Josselyn's *New England Rarities* published in 1672 in which he describes a trip to the crests of the "White Hills" and the view north of "many rich and pregnant valleys as ever the eye beheld, beset on each side with variety of goodly trees; the grass man-high, unmowed." Further, an observation which still would hold true at certain times of the year: "The black flies are so numerous that a man cannot draw his breath but he will suck them in."

It is quite likely that the valleys mentioned were those of the Androscoggin and the Connecticut, both of which could be seen plainly from the crest of any of the Presidential Range mountains.

The process of settlement of the New Hampshire portion of the valley began in late fall of 1770 when Hope Austin decided that Peabody Patent, later called Gilead, was too crowded and he determined before winter set in that he would emigrate further upriver with his family and meager goods. Although it was already cold enough for the trappers' trail which followed the river to be frozen hard, he nevertheless set forth on foot, some say with his wife and small son, a heavy pack on his back and thus heavily laden, his progress was snail-like. After many hours he covered some six miles, crossing the frozen Wild River and what was to become the New Hampshire state border at the end of the Revolution when the colony entered the Union in 1788. In 1770, however, it was a vaguely known border between the Maine district of Massachusetts and the Crown Colony of New Hampshire. At nightfall Austin built a lean-to for shelter on the south bank of the Androscoggin and settled in this neighborhood, though across the river, for the rest of his life. Shortly after Austin settled in Shelburne Daniel Ingalls moved into the town, followed by others in 1772 including Thomas Wheeler, Nathaniel Porter, and Peter Poor.

It is interesting to note, however, that two years before Austin came, a Captain Whipple had come up from Massachusetts and settled in Jefferson, just fourteen miles west of Shelburne, with a party of some dozen others. There was no communication for some years between the two settlements across Gorham Hill, the high point between the watersheds of the Androscoggin and the Connecticut.

Settlement for the next few years was exceedingly slow and did not attain much headway until after the Revolutionary War. By 1780, however, there were perhaps a dozen families scattered up the river in the town of Shelburne and scratching a precarious living from the harsh environment. They were growing grain in the intervales and hunting and fishing for other food and trapping for skins to cover their shivering bodies in the frigid winters. The Revolution hardly touched these isolated areas except for the constant fear of Indian raids from Canada. By 1781 the British, who had taken over Canada from the French at the end of the Seven Years' War, had been inciting the St. Francis Indians to raid in New England. Bounties were offered for scalps and captured settlers and while little of this had been done in the Androscoggin Valley because of the scarcity of settlements, still they had raided all down the Connecticut and the rumors of these depredations were rampant in the colonies, spread by trappers and hunters who used the old Indian trails. On August 5, 1781, six Indians led by one Tomhegan, who was known to most of the settlers as an "impudent red rascal" and had been seen in the vicinity often in the last few years, played havoc with the whole valley starting in Bethel, then known as Sudbury-Canada, where they killed and scalped three men and carried away three others. They raided the homes of these men who had been caught in the fields, gathered all valuables and rum and forced the captives to carry the loot. They halted at the cabin of Peter Austin, a relative of the Shelburne Hope Austin, who was away. They found little of value, but broke some old firearms that were there but did not harm the women and children. At Gilead, they stopped at one Pettingill's house, finding him not at home, they called to him in the field and when he came to the house, they killed him. They did not molest his wife who was ill. At Shelburne they crossed the river to Hope Austin's house. Austin and the children were away and they did not harm Mrs. Austin but it is not hard to believe that the effect on her and the other women was to last for years. The six brawny Indians with the blood-dripping scalps on their belts and the cowering captives were told of for generations in the valley. The raiders were not through however, for Tomhegan knew of the other settlers farther upriver and he alone approached the Ringe homestead and waited in the woods until Peter Poor, an employee of Captain Ringe, and Pluto, his Negro servant, came out to go to the field for work. Tomhegan called to them and beckoned for them to approach. Poor was suspicious and turned to run but Tomhegan shot him in the back, killing him instantly. He then took Pluto with him to the Ringe house where he intimidated the occupants and looted the place, loaded the valuables on the Negro and departed to join the others and started upriver to Lake Umbagog where they had left canoes for the trip back to St. Francis. There they collected their bounties for scalps and the captives who were taken on to Montreal by the British. It is said that the captives all survived sixteen months of captivity and returned to the river valley to live out the rest of their days.

Peter Poor was thought to be the last white man killed by Indians in the entire valley and it may well be so. Just off North Road in Shelburne in a clearing in the woods is a magnificent old white pine tree. It must be two-hundred years old for its girth is about twelve feet at its base. Under its spread, near its trunk, is a granite slab with this epitaph:

Sacred to the memory of
Peter Poor
Shot by an Indian Tom Hegan
and buried on this spot
August 5, 1781

During the last decade of the eighteenth century settlement of the upper valley of the Androscoggin began to pick up. The Revolutionary War was over and as always happens veterans were clamoring for added compensation for their services. The hard-pressed state legislatures were trying to still these clamors by deeding small grants of land in the wilderness to veterans. These men with their families and other adventurous souls, who were dissatisfied for one reason or another with life in the older colonies, migrated to Maine and over into the New Hampshire valley of the Androscoggin. They were a rugged lot and although some could not conquer the vicissitudes of the forest and died or gave up and went back toward the coast, most survived and even flourished. Not only did they survive, but most of them kept moving up the valley until they were satisfied that they had found what they were looking for. It is amazing to find in old records of Bethel and Gilead the same names which appeared a few years later in the records of Shelburne, Gorham, and Berlin, and even in Errol, sixty miles upriver in the wilderness. Thus Maine records names of early settlers of Bethel and Gilead: Thomas Peabody, Captain Joseph Lary, Isaac Adams, Eliphalet Chapman, Captain Eliphalet Burbank, George Burbank, Ephom and Seth Wight, Samuel Wheeler, Henry Philbrook, Evans, and others. All of these names are perpetuated in families of present day Shelburne, Gorham, Berlin, Milan, and Errol.

CHAPTER 14

the
logging era

This progressive settlement
went on during the early years
of the nineteenth century despite hardships of pioneer life and without communication with the outside world. Transportation was difficult and trade was scanty for the few necessities of life which were
not available in the valley. There were, by 1810, a few passable roads to
Lancaster on the Connecticut, to Berlin Falls, then known as Maynesborough, and a long and wearisome trail down from Bethel to Harrison and on to Portland which was a thriving seaport and trading
center for all of Maine and much of New Hampshire. These "roads" for
the most part were mere trails following the old Indian tracks, and
were passable only in summer and then by foot or horseback. A few
wandering peddlers and tinsmiths were beginning to trek through
once or twice a year with gunpowder, utensils, salt, and matches in
their saddlebags.

The War of 1812 had no effect on the valley. There were no Indian or British raids and no troop movements to or from Canada by way of the river. It has been said that the settlers of the upper valley did not even know that the war was being fought until it was over. This was not much of an exaggeration for communication with the coast and with the state government at Concord was practically non-existent until after the end of "Mr. Madison's War."

Life, however, was not a smooth or uninterrupted progression, for harsh and unpredictable hazards dogged their lives. In 1816, early August, there was a catastrophic crop failure caused by snow and freezing temperatures which cut the ordinarily short growing season, and tender plants barely above ground were frost-killed before bearing. By late fall there was famine in the land, but the majority of the settlers survived that miserable winter on forest roots and the remnants of dried and mildewed scrapings from cellar bins and meat stews from the domestic animals, when there was little game. This game scarcity followed quickly after the autumn, for food was as scarce for deer and birds as it was for humans, and the moose in impenetrable bogs, and bears in hibernation were safe from hunters. However, the pioneers survived and new settlers came in and moved upriver.

In 1820 Shelburne had a population of 205. George Green had built a stopover tavern for travelers between Lancaster and Portland, so the roads had apparently improved somewhat. In 1820 the New Hampshire legislature incorporated the town, and a trickling of settlers began to come in from the Connecticut valley where Lancaster was now a thriving town and the uppermost trading point for northern New Hampshire.

Meantime, settlement of Gorham, which was called Shelburne Addition and later, simply Addition, had followed closely on Shelburne. The first settler, one Bezaleel Bennett, arrived in 1803 and was described as "amiable but convivial and indolent, but a good hunter and fisherman." He soon wandered off for it was said he never lived in one place very long. He was followed in 1805 by Stephen Messer of Methuen, Massachusetts, who was in truth the first permanent settler of Addition, and who cleared a farm and reared eleven children.

The creeping northward occupation of the valley did not stop at Shelburne or Addition but proceeded on to Maynesborough which was to become Berlin in 1829. In 1821 William Sessions of Gilead came here and in 1824 built the first house which could be called by this

The Androscoggin becomes a rushing torrent at "The Neck" at Maynesboro (later renamed Berlin Falls) as this mid-nineteenth century photo indicates.

designation. It was on the east bank of the river and he settled here for some years. He was followed by others, most of whom in the early years located above the falls and rapids, for the land immediately around the fast water was far less suitable to farming and householding than the intervales above. Milan too had become a settlement but the source of the migrants was the Connecticut Valley by way of Stratford and Stark. This was natural, for a rough trail had been cut in 1812 across Milan Hill and down the Upper Ammonoosuc River to the Connecticut to join the two valleys. At the beginning of the War of 1812 this was a measure of protection for the citizens of Shelburne and vicinity who were fearful of raids from Canada and presumably it was a connecting link with forts on the Connecticut. The raids did not materialize, but the trail served as a link with Stark, Stratford, and the Connecticut River.

As the valley became sparsely settled during the first three decades of the nineteenth century the beginnings of industrial activity became evident, first with the gristmills being started at Gorham and Berlin and the first usage of water power from the tremendous force of the river and brooks. This was quite an undertaking in itself for grindstones were not available except those made in England and brought over before the Revolution to points on the coast and up the Penobscot River. In fact, the route followed by some of these stones arriving at the Upper Androscoggin was quite remarkable. One set was transported from Bangor by ship to Portland, then by ox cart all the way up to Errol. Most of the others were similarly transported and the expense must have been a terrific burden on such pioneer millers as the Larys of Shelburne and the Greens of Berlin. The latter, Amos and Thomas Green, built the first dam and water facility at Berlin Falls and the freshet of 1826 carried the whole thing away.

In truth, the records of these early industrial pioneers were filled with disaster, but their efforts continued. Almost without exception a mill operation, whether on a contributory brook or the main river, could hope for only a year or two of operation before flood or fire destroyed the enterprise. Nevertheless they persisted, and the coming of the lumber era increased the tempo of sawmill operations all along the upper valley. Small mills were built, mostly on tributary streams near the river, as at Gorham in 1836 on Moose Brook by Jonathan and Andrew Lary, one of the Greens on the Dead River at Jericho, others even as far north as Errol. Most of these little operations were powered by overshot water wheels and up-and-down saws which worked on the seesaw principle and were very slow in operation but were certainly better than hand sawing. Thomas Green, who had earlier been washed out at the Berlin Mills site, moved down to what is now Green Square in the heart of the little city and erected a new mill for up-and-down sawing and a gristmill, using a combination of water power from Dead River and a diversion of the Androscoggin itself. In 1829 his sons, Amos and Daniel, built a clapboard and shingle mill nearby. It burned in 1835, but was rebuilt. However, the Amos Green water privilege, as the power right was called, was in continuous use for mill purposes under a succession of ownerships until 1885 when the Glen Manufacturing Company developed the "great pitch" of the main river and destroyed the usefulness of the Dead River and Green Pond.

The white pine, which was the basis of the tremendous lumber industry of the Penobscot and Kennebec regions, was not as prolific in the New Hampshire valley of the Androscoggin though the early settlers did not realize this, and as a consequence they were recklessly improvident in their methods of cutting and marketing the lumber. The white pine belt was very narrow on each side of the river, usually running only up the lower slopes of the confining mountains, and the same was true of the contributory streams. However, spruce, fir, and a variety of hardwoods were plentiful and became the backbone of the economy when uses for these woods were developed, particularly for pulpwood for paper making. Like the Penobscot and Kennebec lumbermen, the first interest of the early Androscoggin loggers was those beautiful, tall, and straight white pines, for which there was a ready market at Brunswick (and later at Lewiston) where logs were being sawed and lumber shipped all over the world.

Up to this time the sturdy pioneer families of each community supplied the manual labor necessary for the preservation of life in a harsh land. They were combination farmers, woodsmen, carpenters, masons, and mechanics, and skilled in all manner of handicraft. The womenfolk were proficient in the preparation, preservation, and care of food and clothing for the family, and covered such wide fields as first aid and medication, the spinning and weaving of cloth, and the making of soap.

There were no capitalists nor white collar classes and few, if any, had the benefit of more than a rudimentary education, yet they early began to provide some schooling for their children. There was a marked scarcity of gentry in the valley. In fact, with the exception of Captain Whipple of Jefferson, it is doubtful if any settlers of the neighborhood had come into the area with much more than the clothes on their backs and the contents of a gunny sack or two and the pioneer spirit of "make out with what you've got."

Now, with a modicum of security having been achieved and the roads having been improved to the extent that some communication was possible with the coasts and "civilization," the more ambitious and ingenious of the pioneers began to look at the enormous possibilities of the forest with an eye to profit and further improvement in their primitive conditions. In addition, capitalists, in the form of men of substance from Portland and other coastal towns, had begun to eye the untapped forests of the valley and to make trips into the area with the view of beginning lumbering operations by local men with guarantees of a market for logs at tidewater. In turn, this led to the introduction of the second class which had been lacking in the society of the valley, a specialized type of laborers, the logger and river driver. This was one class, not two, and it differed in many ways from the pioneer settler class. First, the logger was not a family man, nor was he of strictly English colonial stock. He was a breed of his own and a colorful breed too. He was usually single and he might be a younger son of a pioneer family who saw no advantage in staying at home when there was no prospect for gain or land. He might be an Irish immigrant off a boat at Boston and lured with an offer of free transportation to the big woods by an agent for lumbering interests in Portland or Bangor. He could be anyone in the way of a rough, tough, handyman with an axe from Norway, Sweden, or Russia who had no family in America and was rugged enough to like the wild, hard life of a logger and river man. They were transients, not settlers, and many of the early ones would grow restless after a "season of lumberin' " on the Penobscot, move to the Kennebec for a time and then to the Androscoggin and the Connecticut and later to Michigan and on westward, ever following the dwindling virgin pine.

The primary economic law of supply and demand holds true, of course, in any industrial development. Although in the early days there was an ample supply of timber and a sure market for long logs at the coast by shipbuilders and sawmills, still that market was beset with difficulties of transporting logs over a hundred miles of wild and temperamental river, and the farmer-logger of the valley simply did not have the knowledge or the financial resources to tackle it successfully. On the other hand there was a local market for some lumber, clapboard, and shingles for the growing rural communities, but the

Early industrial development had its problems; above grist mills at Rumford in 1865 and below, the same location following the first power dam-log jam in 1891.

surplus must be laboriously hauled in summertime by ox teams to Harrison, Maine, some forty miles over make-shift roads. From Harrison it was loaded on boats and carried deviously through lakes and canals until it finally arrived at Portland. The cost of this transport was high but it did furnish to the do-it-yourself lumbermen a cash crop which was necessary for any further development of their mills.

Now that the coastal capital was becoming interested in the Androscoggin, it was not necessary to look too far for the second class of society which the valley lacked, the logger and river man. Thus it was to the Kennebec and the Penobscot that the budding lumber industry turned, for in the late thirties and forties Bangor was the capital of the world in lumbering and the birthplace of all logging in the United States. Ships crowded her docks, and mills lined the river banks from Bucksport up through Bangor and Old Town for forty miles on the Penobscot, and the Kennebec was not far behind. The very nature of the lumberjack made it easy to recruit him for the Androscoggin, for his philosophy, as Stewart Holbrook so vividly describes in his books on New England lumbering was, "let the daylight into the swamp, drive the river down to town, get your teeth fixed, then over the hump to the next job." The term "getting your teeth fixed" was a euphemism for two weeks of "painting the town red," or until a season's wages were spent. Here a recruiter would tell of the marvels of cutting on the Androscoggin where the white pine was so thick that it blotted out the sun, the exciting drives, and the saloons and brothels of Errol, Berlin, Lewiston, and Brunswick which were like paradise itself.

The first drives were hazardous and not too successful operations for there were not enough real river men available and no dams for water control. The drives had a way of running out of water before they got halfway and in summertime the river was so blocked by jams in many places that it took nearly two seasons to drive the logs to tidewater. In spring freshet time when the ice went out there was little difficulty, but there were plenty of physical hazards in riding the long sticks down the stretches between rapids and falls. On the approach to Berlin and Rumford Falls a logger had to be very agile either to ride the fast water or get off and follow on the banks. The peril of log jams and the untangling of them at the falls was a stupendous job, particularly before 1858 when Joe Peavey, of Bangor, invented his "Peavey" Cant Dog, an implement which made the great drives of later years possible.

The drives continued, however, every spring with logs cut in the dead of winter and sledded, "snaked," or skidded by ox power out of the woods to the river and on to the ice to wait "break up" in the spring thaw. The woodsmen began to come up the river in the fall to work until the drives ended in Brunswick and Lewiston in the spring. Here they would be paid off and would head for the nearest saloons and brothels, and when broke, go "over the hump" to new swamps that needed "daylight let into 'em." Sometimes this was the Connecticut River, Tupper Lake in New York, or further west.

Thus during the two decades between 1830 and mid-century the valley made fairly steady progress in the growth of its little communities and their economic development. In 1836 Gorham was incorporated as a town with some 135 inhabitants. Shelburne had some 400 people (which incidentally probably exceeds today's population), and Berlin, which held its first town meeting in 1829, had a population of seventy-two, of which fifteen were voters. Settlers were continuing to come up the valley, clearing land and planting in the intervales as far north as Wentworth Location on the Magalloway. In addition the population was swelled periodically by the new breed, the logger-river drivers, who came up in the fall and into the dense woods for the winter's work. Transient though this migration was, it added to the prosperity of the communities, for the native Yankee acumen quickly grasped the possibilities of the annual descent of several hundred "Bangor Tigers" on the settlements as the drive went through on the river.

There was profit to be derived in hauling supplies up to the woods camps, and at the peak of the cutting, before the pine began to dwindle, there was a continuous stream of heavy, double-team oxen rigs going upriver, wagons in summer and sleds in winter. Taverns and "hotels" were erected to take care of the "fixing of teeth" of the loggers when they burst loose from the isolation of the deep woods.

At the same time certain activity was taking place in Boston and Portland which would give the valley its really great boost in development. It was the beginning of railroad building. By 1842 a rail line had reached from Boston to Portsmouth, New Hampshire, and two years later to Portland, Maine. In 1847 the Atlantic and St. Lawrence Railway was chartered, and its promoters, Josiah Little and his Portland associates, among whom were J.B. Brown, and Nathan and Hezekiah Winslow, were authorized to construct a railroad from Portland to Montreal by way of Auburn (then called Danville) and following the Little Androscoggin and the main river to Gorham, then westerly to the Connecticut River and into lower Canada. The original route did not include Berlin Falls but it is quite probable, in view of the later activities of the four men mentioned above, that they had already seen the power possibilities of the river at that point and had personal designs on the acquisition of the water rights, if rail transportation were assured.

By the latter part of 1848 the Atlantic and St. Lawrence Railroad was completed from Portland to Mechanic Falls on the Little Androscoggin River with a connection to Auburn. From there it pushed on rapidly up the valley through Norway, South Paris, West Paris and joining the main river at Bethel. Still following the river, the rails reached Gorham in 1851, amid the rejoicing of the population. Not only was there now fast transportation to the market places of the coast, but Gorham had been designated as the location of the railway shops and a division point between the projected route to Canada. Excitement in the town was rampant for the actual building of the rail line had brought money, cash money, a previously scarce article, in the form of payrolls. It was said that the influx of permanent citizens had accelerated all along the line from the coast, due to the number of laborers settling in each spot as the line progressed. This excitement followed upriver to Berlin for it was decided in 1853 to route the rails through that town and swing northwest at that point on its way to Stratford on the Connecticut River and up to join the Grand Trunk Railway on the Canadian border at Island Pond, Vermont.

About this time a syndicate of Portland men began to buy up land at the "neck" in Berlin where the river pinches tightly between granite walls at the beginning of the rapids forming Berlin Falls. This was the same site that Thomas Green had attempted to use for his mill in 1826 and which had been washed out by the first freshet. The group was eventually to become the firm of H. Winslow & Company, and the names of the partners were Josiah Little, J.B. Brown, and Nathan and Hezekiah Winslow of Portland, Maine. The Winslow Company was the first of a series of well-financed but absentee ownership concerns to bring large-scale industry to the upper Androscoggin valley.

It immediately began to build a very modern sawmill with a dam for power and water control and at the same time practically eliminated the costly, long, river drives of logs to the coast. When completed the Winslow Company and their successors would be able to saw and ship all of the lumber products cut above Berlin Falls. The first mill contained one gang and two single saws with a daily capacity of

25,000 feet of long lumber, a fabulous figure for the day and location. The effect of these activities on the people of the towns of Shelburne, Gorham, and Berlin was immediate. Shelburne assumed its quiet role of a rural community, with little change in population to this day. There was practically no industry but farming, except for a small mill which had been washed out several times at the great rocks and a little flurry of mining excitement when Amos Peabody, in 1846, interested outside capital in a lead mine he had discovered in 1820 on the side of the Mahoosic Range above his farm place. A small smelter was built but the project was abandoned in 1849. It was reopened briefly in 1880 and operated for a little while and again abandoned. The shaft, now filled with water from the brook at its side, is still visible, and the solid brick entrance is a monument to the enterprise. Shelburne continued as a way station for settlers who, after a while, moved upriver to the growing activity in Gorham and Berlin.

Meanwhile Gorham had become a boom town and business places were opening to take care of the needed supplies of a growing population and a new class of transients, the railroad travelers. Several small hotels were erected and shortly after the railroad station was completed the Alpine House was built at an unheard-of cost of $20,000. Gorham had assumed its long-to-be held place as the gateway to the White Mountains. Now, in addition to the construction workers, there were sightseers and summer visitors coming to view the suddenly accessible Presidential Range of the White Mountains.

In 1851 on the stage road which led up through Pinkham Notch and connected Gorham with the Eastern Slope towns of Jackson and Conway, John Bellows of Exeter erected a public house in "The Glen." It was at the base of the carriage road which had been built to the crest of Mount Washington. This hostelry, and its successors, were to serve visitors to the area for over a hundred years. Most of them came to Gorham on the new rail line and were transported to the Glen House by stage. The Mount Washington carriage trips to the crest began here. The Glen Houses, under a succession of owners, were built and destroyed by fire four times during one hundred and sixteen years of existence.

The first fire, in 1884, leveled what had become a tremendous structure, over four hundred feet long. It was rebuilt even larger during 1885-1886 and stood only seven years before it burned in 1893 with a loss of a quarter million dollars. The third edition of the hostelry, built by adding to the old servants' quarters which had been saved from the fire, was erected by the firm of E. Libby and Sons, Company, of Gorham, who had acquired the property. This building was to last longer, despite the Glen House nemesis, for it was not destroyed until 1924. The third building, on a much smaller scale than its predecessors, lasted even longer and burned in March of 1967 at the height of the ski season. At that time the owners, the Libby heirs, announced that the Glen House was finished forever as a hotel and that possibly a modern motel of a hundred or so units would be built on the historic site.

The mills which had been built on the Peabody and Moose Rivers were becoming important additions to the economy of the town, for rail shipments of finished lumber products to the coast were making sound business concerns of the former marginal operations. The moral tone of the community began to change with the influx of new people, and while there had been scattered religious meetings held by traveling Free Will Baptists preaching as early as 1815, it was not until 1856 that formal church services were held by Congregational ministers, by Methodists in 1858, and Universalists a few years later. Schools, however, had been maintained since 1823 when Miss Salome Mason was hired as teacher for the magnificent stipend of $1.00 per week and room and board.

The population figures for the towns in the upper valley were quite misleading for they were based upon permanent citizens and their families and never, until modern times, reflected the actual populace, for the very nature of the economy of the two basic industries, wood products and tourism, created a floating seasonal and transient population until the twentieth century.

In Berlin the arrival of the rail line also caused much excitement and bustling activity as workmen for the new mill came to town. Housing had to be prepared and this took the form of what was to be a north country institution, the boarding house or "Hotel" for transient workers. Accommodations were needed for the mechanics and carpenters employed in the building of the dam and mill, but principally for the hordes of woodsmen who would make the town their base for the cutting of millions of board feet of lumber and the spring river drives from the forests of the Diamonds, the Magalloway, and the Maine Lakes country. The first of these large houses was built in 1853 by the Winslow Company for the foremen and engineers in charge of the construction work. At the same time the first section of the company store was erected. In the meantime several small retail establishments were constructed for services which had been lacking in the pioneer town: cobbler and shoe making shops, smithies, and general stores which handled everything from hay and grain to needles and pins. As temperance was not a general virtue in the valley, there were taverns and rum shops which supplied bottled goods in sufficiency.

This was one of the first examples of industrial paternalism in America. The single industry, consisting of the Winslow Company and its successors, the Berlin Mills Company, the Brown Company, and for a while the International Paper Company, dominated the life of the community in practically all of its activities for many years. It was a paternalistic relationship in its better sense, in accordance with the business ethics of the day. True, the company exerted pressures politically and financially in order to get what it believed to be best, not only for themselves but for the community, which they knew constituted the same thing. However, there was little opposition to these ideas by the people of Berlin for they were eternally grateful for the introduction of a measure of economic security which had been unknown in the area previously.

These men, although absentee owners, were nevertheless highly skilled and experienced in organizing a business. They hired men who were thoroughly trained in the rough and tumble of lumbering as it had been practiced on the Penobscot and Kennebec for years and immediately began operations for "getting the wood out" and to supply the new mill when it would be ready for manufacturing. Cruisers had been tramping the woods upriver for months before the syndicate had even secured the water rights at Berlin Mills Village which was springing up at the "neck," a mile or so above Berlin Falls.

Recruiters had been busy on the Penobscot signing up woods bosses and river men for the coming winter and passing the word in Bangor saloons that there were "new swamps" up the Androscoggin. All of these embellishments appealed to the migratory instinct of the lumberjacks and this characteristic took them not only to the Androscoggin but all the way across the continent to Washington and Oregon after cutting a swath hundreds of miles wide through the northern woods.

Soon after the cruisers had finished their first surveys another group of specialists came to build the first camps for the winter's work. These men were known as woods butchers and they were actually artists with the axe, saw, and auger. They went into the woods with a few swampers to clear the camp sites and start on woods "roads" for hauling logs from stump to river, then proceeded to build the camps and all of the furnishings necessary to feed and shelter forty to a hundred men who would be "snowed in" for four to six months. These furnishings were simple but the "woods butcher" took pride in his work and the camp itself, and the "hovel" or stable for the oxen and horses was snugly built of logs with moss caulking.

The first woods camps were rather crude affairs but they served the purpose admirably in their primary functions of providing shelter against the bitter cold of winter and feeding facilities for man and beast. The writer was hunting in northern Maine in the fall of 1940 with a friend and his great uncle, who admitted to being eighty-five years of age, at least sixty-five of which had been spent in the woods. He had been a logger, camp boss, and walking boss for one of the big lumbering outfits and later for paper companies, on the Penobscot, Kennebec, Androscoggin, and Connecticut rivers. Old Jack Harris was as spry as a man in his thirties and could out-walk both his nephew, Charlie Harris, who was thirty-six and the writer who was about the same age. We came to a clearing, partially grown up and there was a low log structure in the center of the cleared spot. Old Jack walked up to the sagging doorway and pointed to a moss covered inscription carved in the still solid oak door frame. It had the letters D.P. and the numerals 70-71 inscribed. We looked from the inscription to old Jack who was smiling.

Charlie said, "What's that mean, Uncle, Jack?"

"Well, you boys wouldn't know, but this here camp was the first camp I ever worked at. That there D.P. is Dave Pingree who we was cuttin' for and them dates was the winter of 1870 and '71 and she was an old Christer of a winter, too. I was cookee and camp boy doin' the bull cookin' too."

He pushed open the door and we went inside. It was like a dank cave and one of the most depressing sights the author ever beheld, but the walls of eighteen inch logs were still tight. Then Jack told us that he regularly, once or twice a year, came by the old camp and "battened her down" and patched up holes that might have appeared on the roof. It was used occasionally by hunters who were lost in the woods or delayed by weather and while it was only five miles from the road where we had left the car, it might have been a hundred miles from civilization. Jack went on to tell us that he had put a new roof on the building back in 1910 when he was woods boss for International Paper Company in a season when they were cutting in the neighborhood.

"I had the boys replace the rail rafters in her and slap on some tar paper, but other than that she's just the way she was in that first winter."

Then he called attention to the bunks and crude furniture and said they had been there all of this time too. When asked why he had taken care of the old camp through all of those years he said, "Dunno, jest wanted to see how long the old barsted 'ud stand, I guess."

The original roof on the structure had been bark, later replaced with handmade shingles. The building was about fifty feet long by twenty wide and there were no windows. Originally there had been a hole in the middle of the roof for the smoke from a sand-based fireplace in the center of the room. This furnished all of the heat and also was used for cooking. The utensils originally had been pots and kettles hanging from swinging cranes. Sometime, probably in 1910 when Jack had replaced the roof, an old and battered Franklin stove had been substituted for the fireplace and the smoke went out a rusty pipe through the side of the building. The old smoke hole had been covered. The bunks which ran along the entire back wall and consisted of two tiers were muzzle loaders — you had to climb over the foot to get into them. This particular camp, so Jack told us, had housed ninety-five men. Charlie smiled and said, "Must have been a bit cozy."

"Yeah," said old Jack, "and when supper was done and there was a roarin' fire in the grate, and all the wet clothes was hangin' around and steamin', and near a hundred sweaty woods rats in their long johns was settin' on the deacon seat or hangin' out of bunks with their boots off, it were a mite smelly. But you got used to it."

The "deacon seat" was a necessity in all woods camps in those days. It was simply the split half of a fifty-foot log on peg legs which ran along the foot of the bunks and was fashioned entirely with a broadaxe but the top of this one was as smooth as a piano finish. Certainly most of this high polishing was done by several hundred hard "Bangor tiger" tails, which had buffed the wood during those bitter winters in the seventies when the camp was in full use.

While this particular camp was located on the headwaters of the Kennebec, the building specifications and furnishings were apparently identical with those first camps built on the Upper Androscoggin and throughout the North Woods.

The old woodsmen are gone but their tales linger on as folklore with the people of Maine and New Hampshire. Yes, gone with old

Jack Harris who died in his early nineties as he would have wished. His old heart simply stopped one December day as he hauled a little doe back over the trail from the deep woods near his home where he had shot the animal. The snow was deep and his snowshoes were biting into the steep grade when suddenly it was all over. He had a good life doing what he wanted to do and dying as he would have liked, quickly, in his beloved woods.

Not only had the camp construction been uniform, but the actual methods of logging were so much the same that a woodsman was instantly at home in a new location and in fact was hardly conscious of where his woods were located. Of course the spring drive down the river was different for each stream, but the bosses usually had experience on all of them and there were enough local men on the crews to take the rapids and falls in their stride.

Woods methods of cutting and hauling to the river remained about the same for fifty years and the tools for felling were the broadaxe and the single bit axe. The camp foreman would assign his cutters to a section of woods and generally, unless he had full confidence in his cutters, would mark the trees to be felled with an axe "blaze." This selectivity was simply for size as the woodsmen of the era were not interested in leaving anything but stumps in the cutover area, and "letting the daylight into the swamp" was not only the religion of the lumberjack, but that of the logging business itself. It was not until the twentieth century that foresters and forward-looking conservationists entered the business and began the practice of selective cutting and tree farming which has brought the forests back to northern New England.

The personnel of the camps included a few specialists, but was made up for the most part of axemen with a camp foreman or "Bull of the Woods" who exercised complete control over all activities except that of the cook who was boss of meals and mealtime and where no conversation was allowed. His helpers, before the separation of the barrooms (or bunk houses) from the cook house, which occurred after a few years, were the cookees (kitchen and dining helpers) and the bull-cook, who was in fact janitor and fire tender. It gradually became the rule when camps were a little better organized, for a separate shack to be erected for cooking and eating. After that the bull-cook was responsible only for the barroom and fires and the fuel for them, while the cook was lord of his realm. If he was good his reputation insured his solicitation by many woods bosses each season.

About an hour before sun up the bull-cook or a cookee would beat on a dish pan and bellow "Day-a-light in the swaammp" and up they'd get, growling and hawking, and grab their now dry shirts and pants, don their boots and go to breakfast. This meal was the same as supper in the old days, beans, salt pork, bread and molasses and tea "strong enough to float an axe" to wash it all down. Variety in food did not improve much until the twentieth century, but the quantity was always sufficient. Lunch or "dinner," as it was called, was the same if the cutters were working close enough to camp to come in for their "nooning," but if not, they took a cold lunch with them and ate at the "stump." The average day's work was fourteen hours and it was rugged and cold work six days a week. Sunday was usually spent repairing boots and clothing and grinding and honing axes to a razor's edge. This was not a misnomer for those few woods rats who were "dudes" actually shaved with their axes occasionally, with a lather from strong lye soap! They were a tough crew, these early loggers. When supper was over and they had shed their wet clothing and boots and smoked a pipe, they fell into bunks and in moments they were gone for ten hours of noisy coma. For, as old Jack Harris said, "If you never heard a hundred ole woods rats a snorin' in chorus, you never heard nothin'."

It was no wonder that when the cutting and the river drive were over, these men, isolated in remote woods for six months or more at backbreaking labor, with no social contacts, and recreation consisting of exhausted unconsciousness, were ready to break out when they hit town with a pocket full of money. They were not paid until the season ended and in fact had no use for money in the woods, all room and board being furnished and the wangan taking care of what personal supplies they needed in camp. This wangan (no one knows where the term came from) was simply a storage place for tools (axes), tobacco, boots, and clothes, and sometimes soap. Here the men could "draw" against wages, and in the early camps, it was in the hands of the foreman and later the camp clerk.

This, then, was the kind of woods operation which the "brass" at H. Winslow & Company organized and put into operation in the Thirteen Mile Woods on the banks of the Androscoggin shortly after the railroad arrived at Berlin. The industrial development of the upper valley was begun.

An additional element in the development of the wood resources of the valley had now entered the picture, and like all of the know-how of the business, had trickled over from the experienced and shrewd lumber and river barons of the Penobscot. These people had found out that the control of water transportation was essential to profitable operation of New England's woodlands. In fact, quite a few fortunes had been accumulated by Bangor, Veazy, and Old Town, Maine, "water people." They did not have to buy or lease huge tracts of woodland, finance year-long operations of hundreds of cutters with the necessary expense of camp building and maintenance, or put up expensive mills and equip them with costly machinery to make a "dollar in the lumberin' business." In fact, all that was necessary was the acquisition of "water rights" at key points on those sections of a river which required or indicated dams for the control of water heights or pitch for getting the logs through with the least difficulty. Then if you were to build a dam or series of dams in fast water, with gates to control water levels and the passage of logs, you were in business, and a very profitable business it was. Charges were made per hundred logs of passage and if you were dependent on your supply of logs from above, you paid the required passage fees.

The water "pirates" of the Penobscot and Kennebec Rivers were running out of water in the middle of the century and were looking for new territory for their profitable sideline. However, a new influence was being felt here and there along the Androscoggin. In 1852 the New Hampshire Legislature chartered the Androscoggin River Improvement Company of Errol, New Hampshire, but the strange thing was that the organizers were E. S. Coe of Bangor and L.E. Dunn of Old Town, Maine (both towns being on the Penobscot River).

The records of these transactions are rather hazy and the reasons shrouded in obscurity but it is understandable as the loggers themselves rather resented the intrusion of the watermen on their profit picture. Exactly what arrangements the Winslow people made in order to get their logs from the Parmachenee and Rangeley Lakes areas is not known but they were apparently unable to gain the outright control of the dams which was essential to their (and their successors') profitable operations, until late in the nineteenth century. Meantime, they probably paid "through the nose" to the "water people." Prior to 1858 there were two dams built by others than Winslow: at Upper and Middle on the lakes beside the Errol Dam. As late as 1876 there is record of the Errol Dam Company, organized by R.C. Pingree, George S. Bearse, E.S. Coe, David Pingree, and L.E. Dunn, all of whom were citizens of Penobscot towns or of Lewiston on the Lower Androscoggin, and none were connected with Winslow or its first successor, the Berlin Mills Company.

The Errol Dam Company was purchased by The Union Water Power Company after its incorporation in 1878 in connection with the City of Lewiston agreement mentioned previously.

CHAPTER 15

industrial

beginnings

During the quarter century from 1850 to the middle of the seventies the development of the New Hampshire valley of the river was almost static. The sudden growth caused by the coming of the railroad had taken place almost overnight and lumbering, the primary and single industry, was slowly enveloping the entire upper valley and Maine headwaters, as far as actual logging was concerned. However the labor requirements at the mills themselves did not increase proportionately.

Although sawing equipment was added to the Winslow Mill in 1855 and 1858, the personnel of the mill itself did not increase greatly and it was possible for thirty-five or so employees to saw and process the production of several hundred woodsmen who were strictly transients. Even the addition finally in 1860 of rotary saws in the mill, which vastly increased the output but not the labor requirements, did not noticeably swell the permanent population of Berlin, which in that year was nearly 400. However, the periodic appearance of about the same number of loggers and river men did so contribute to the economy that the business section along the river front appeared to be that of a much larger town.

The outbreak of the Civil War, and in fact its whole course, had little effect on the upper valley or its economy except that the tremendous demand for lumber for ships and other uses kept the industry humming. While there was some difficulty with manpower shortages, the contribution of actual citizenry to the army was rather small and from Berlin itself the proportion of purchased substitutions during the drafts was high. The records show only nineteen three-year men, thirteen one-year men and three nine-months' men serving in the army. It is not known how many of these were duplications, for certainly some did extend their enlistments, but not over thirty-five of the population, at most, served in the uniformed services during the four years of the conflict. Gorham, on the other hand, sent proportionately many more of her sons to serve, and this was true of Shelburne and the other rural towns further downriver. However, it can be said that the early settlers did contribute most heavily and the enlistment names of Green, Jordan, Bean, Tuttle, and Lary were numerous and they were all of the old original families who had migrated up through Shelburne to Berlin, and not the Johnnies-come-lately brought in with the railroad.

In 1866, just after the close of the war, a man who was to have a vast influence on the whole upper valley, though he never actually lived in the north country bought into the Winslow Company. This man was William Wentworth Brown and he was at that time living in Portland where he had just closed out a very profitable business which he realized was to become obsolete in a very few years. It might be said here that this foresight was the characteristic which was to have a great influence on the economy of the valley. W. W. Brown was in the business of manufacturing ships' knees, mostly from hardwood, in Bangor, but had moved his business to Portland in 1850 in order to have more accessible supplies of his particular kind of timber in a less competitive market. He prospered in his new location but after the appearance of the Monitor and the Merrimac in the naval engagements of the Civil War he realized that the day of the wooden ship was waning. He very shrewdly sold out and grasped the opportunity of buying into a going and promising business. The Winslows were quite old and had made sufficient fortunes to want to get out of the enterprise. Mr. Little had died shortly after completing his railroad and leasing to the Grand Trunk, so W. W. Brown, Mrs. J. S. Little, and several others from Portland formed a partnership under the name of the Berlin Mills Company and under "W. W." things began to hum more vigorously than ever. For his times he must have been a very shrewd and efficient executive for he managed from his office in Portland what actually became an industrial complex before his death, although located a hundred miles away. True, he sired able sons who did come to Berlin and manage the various phases of the business, but the old gentleman himself was, as one of his longtime employees said, "Always with a finger in the pie," and he was speaking not only of the Berlin Mills Company but the many, many square miles of woodlands which the company controlled and the very life and certainly the politics of the upper valley of the Androscoggin River.

In 1868 W. W. bought out the other partners in the business and with Lewis T. Brown owned the whole "shebang." On L. T.'s death in '78, the ownership of W. W. Brown and his sons became exclusive and lasted for over fifty years.

The Berlin Mills Company steadily progressed during the next five years and when the depression of 1873-1878 hit the country, W. W. Brown simply slowed down operations until it was over. The nature of the seasonal operations in the woods allowed this slowdown without much effect on the economy of the towns except to cut down the influx of the woodsmen twice a year. W. W. was convinced that prosperity and a demand for his wood products would come back, and in 1888 the company was incorporated since it had become too large and unwieldy to be handled as a partnership or individual ownership. However, controlling stock remained with W. W. Brown and his sons, and one of the sons, Herbert, moved to Berlin as superintendent of operations. In this way absentee ownership and management became a thing of the past, and except for the fact that W. W. was still running the business from Portland, the company was directed almost entirely locally.

Meantime the Browns were watching a new development on the river at Berlin. This was the arrival from Pennsylvania of H. H. Furbish. He had been experimenting actively with a new method of making pulp for papermaking with the soda process. The Forest Fiber Company was organized and built a plant on the river for making the product. It was a small plant and produced only six tons of pulp per day. This was in July of 1877, and several years later the capacity had increased to twenty-five tons, but technical difficulties in the use of poplar wood developed. The process was never completely satisfactory, and with the perfection of the sulfite process by Tilghman in 1887, the method became obsolete and the Furbish mills were shut down. It is another indication of the sagacity of W. W. Brown that he did not go into the soda process of pulp making but waited for the sulfite process, though he had become convinced some years before that his operation would eventually go into pulp.

In 1870 the manufacture of paper was done almost entirely with rags with some admixture of straw and mechanically ground wood, though very little of the latter which was produced by only one mill at Stockbridge, Massachusetts. The industry was seeking improvements in pulp, particularly the desired uniformity and possible lower cost which was improbable with rags. By 1881 a few groundwood plants had been started in the East and in that year the first one was built by the Umbagog Paper Company at Livermore Falls, down the river in Maine, of which Hugh J. Chisholm of Portland was the moving spirit. This man will be heard of much more for he was to become, with W. W. Brown, the second of the two most influential figures in the economic development of the Upper Androscoggin Valley.

In 1883 the White Mountain Pulp and Paper Company was organized and its management purchased the old Daniel Green location and river privilege at the mouth of the Dead River in Berlin, using the same methods of waterpower that Green had used for many years in his saw and gristmill. Here they built the first groundwood mill to be erected in New Hampshire. They operated this mill with additions for some four years before selling out to the Glen Manufacturing Company which had been operating since 1885 at the "great pitch" of the river just across and slightly downstream from the Green location. The Glen Company was an organization of Boston and Haverhill, Massachusetts, capitalists, and the operating personnel which they brought with them also introduced a thorough knowledge of the groundwood business and the manufacture of newsprint paper, the demand for which had developed an insatiable market since the Civil War. Now W. W. Brown decided to act on his hunch which had been simmering since 1870 and as soon as his incorporation was completed, he built his first groundwood pulp mill. This was the Riverside Mill and was upriver near his lumber operation at Berlin Mills. As soon as this operation was in full force he began installing paper machines across the river in the Riverside Paper Mill for the manufacture of newsprint, using the Glen Company processes of rag and ground-wood and, it was whispered, some key process men who had been persuaded to move upriver a mile or so. Now that he had again been committed to a new business he did not rest on his laurels but gained a few months on his rival, Glen, by starting the Burgess Sulphite Fibre Company of which he was the largest stockholder. They immediately began construction on a mill for producing sulfite pulp in 1892. Glen's sulfite mill was built in the following year and ended the necessity of importing tons of rags to Berlin. Sulfite pulp obviated that need and from that time on all of the raw materials for the many millions of tons of rolled paper which were to be shipped all over the world, were produced in the valley, from the tree to the maws of the great presses of metropolitan newspapers.

In 1898 Glen Manufacturing Company entered the newly formed International Paper Company, a combination of twenty paper mills scattered in Maine, Vermont, Massachusetts, New Hampshire, and upper New York State, formed for mutual advantages in marketing their product, newsprint paper.

This was not only the beginning of a new era in the economy of the valley, but the start of serious industrial river pollution which increased yearly for half a century before public outcry against its continual worsening caused a beginning of action for the recovery of the river to its former usefulness as a thing of beauty and utility, rather than the vile, lifeless, stinking sewer which it became in the 1940's. Unfortunately the sulfite process of pulping, which was such a god-send to the paper industry, created useless waste liquors laden with oxygen-devouring chemicals and insoluble sediment which gradually covered the river bottom, destroying the water vegetation which is so necessary to water life and to the natural "self purification" which the mill operators said would take care of their sewage.

The river had become, in the eighties, simply a means of transport for logs in the spring, and the conveniently accessible open sewer for communal waste, for steam had replaced its power function and not until the further development of waterpower for electricity was it used for anything else. The replacement of direct waterpower by steam was natural, for with the immense supply of wood for fuel the transition to the more efficient power source was inevitable. In addition the coming of chemical processes for cooking the pulp with acid in the huge converters made the production of heat mandatory.

In the fifteen years from the end of the Civil War to 1880, the population of the little town of Berlin had been steadily increasing each year and had reached about 1,150 souls. In the twenty years to the end of the century it was to balloon to the respectable figure of nearly nine thousand, and there were certain ethnic changes taking place also.

The changes in personnel of the woodsmen first began to be evident in the late sixties and seventies and it was the need to fill a manpower shortage that caused it. The old Yankee loggers and rivermen had been subject for a long time to the blandishments of moving on over the next hump, and what Stewart Holbrook called the "Yankee Exodus" in his book of the same title, was in full swing. Hardly a year went by that New England crews of woodsmen were not decimated by this phenomenon, and the answer to the query of "Where is ole High-pockets Gallager, ain't he workin' this year?" was "Naw, he went to York State [or Michigan or Minnesota]."

Nevertheless the crews had to be filled, and Scotch Irish from New Brunswick, "P.I.'s" (Prince Edward Islanders) and the beginning of French Canadians from Quebec Province, were soon employed. The Maritime Province men were known as "Blue Noses" and "Herring Pickers" and the Frenchmen as "Canucks" or "Pea Soupers," but they were all good in the woods and perhaps the Canucks were the best. At least they lasted longer and were not attracted to the western exodus like the Yankees. A rugged group of Scandinavians—Danes, Norwegians and Swedes—began to trickle into the Androscoggin valley during the eighties.

These workers were generally a little more stable in character than the old Yankee woods rat in that there was a greater proportion of married men who wanted to raise their children in the area and this was also true of the Scots and the Scandinavians. The French too, usually had family ties at home, and while they were willing to come down into Maine and New Hampshire for the "season" they wanted to get back in spring for planting their little farms and "catching up on their home work." Of course there were many wild ones among the newcomers, but unlike the old crews they were not all willing to spend their entire winter's pay on a week or two of wild "teeth fixing." In fact, there were still enough of the old breed left to light up the town when the season ended and the floors of the "hotels" and saloons were well perforated each year with calk marks and there still was much broken glass and furniture to clean up when the last dollar had been spent.

While the vast majority of the new emigrants were attracted to the upper valley by the recruiting activities of the woods bosses, there was still another class of workmen who were brought in for their skills in carpentry and mechanics for the building of the mills, and after their completion for the operation of the complicated machinery which was being installed. Many of these people came directly from the boats which were unloading from Europe in the great surge of immigration during the last quarter of the nineteenth century, and they came to Berlin on transportation advanced by the labor recruiters. The Swedes and Norwegians came because they were told that northern New England was similar to their own Scandinavian countrysides, the Irish and Scotch from New Brunswick because the economy of their harsh land was at a low ebb, and the French Canadians because the forest cutting was so much better organized than yet had been possible in their own lands and cash wages were badly needed to supplement the scanty proceeds of their farms for the support of their constantly growing families.

The proportion of individuals who went into the woods, as opposed to those who settled in the towns and worked in the mills, was about the same for all of the ethnic groups, with the wild and adventuresome ones choosing the woods, while the more domesticated chose the towns with steady wages and a home and family to come back to each evening.

The economic development of the valley was closely followed by cultural and spiritual developments in the towns, with churches and schools being organized and the sons of some of the more prosperous families even being sent away to Dartmouth, Bowdoin, and one or two even to hallowed Harvard. The valley was becoming civilized to the extent of some frowning on the demon rum and the brawling of woodsmen as they came through after the cutting season. This reform did not go so far as to hinder the woods operation. The industrial tycoons could not allow that, for while they contributed liberally to both schools and churches there were no effective blue laws enacted.

In Berlin the arrival of the new nationalities soon became evident, though the Scandinavians rather kept to themselves in the beginning to the extent of settling in what became known as the Scandinavian Village or Swedetown, as the irreverent were apt to call it. In 1887 they organized St. Paul's Lutheran Church, and shortly thereafter became integrated into the life of the town. Neilsens, Nelsons, Olesens, and Petersons began to appear on the voting lists, business firms, and school enrollments, as well as on payroll lists in the mills and woodlands.

To a greater extent the French gathered in their own community, largely on the east side of the river, and for many years retained their native language in everyday use. Shortly after the turn of the century the Catholic churches organized parochial schools which for years taught English as a foreign language.

The Irish and Scotch almost immediately infiltrated the Yankee community and maintained no old-world affiliations as such except for their membership in the various churches which had sprung up in the last twenty years of the century.

The Irish, first, had organized St. Anne's Catholic Church in 1881, only predated by the Congregational Church of 1876, which was of course predominantly Yankee. However, the French Canadians began to flock in and swarmed to St. Anne's in such numbers that a French priest was sent there in 1885 and services were held mostly in French. The Irish revolted and formed St. Kiernans in 1894 and it is known to this day as the Irish Catholic Church, and English, with the usual Latin, became the language for services.

The final event of the century which proudly marked the progress of Berlin was the passage in the New Hampshire General Court of a bill establishing the City of Berlin at a town meeting held in February, 1899, calling for a vote on the new city charter which was adopted. It is interesting to note that the petitioners for this town meeting and the officers elected contained the names of French derivation such as Cote, Beaudoin, Lambert, Letourneau, as well as an Oleson, and such old Yankee, Scotch and Irish names as Wilson, Clarke, Burbank, Marston, Day, Daley, and McHugh. The melting pot was in evidence.

CHAPTER 16

the

Mid Valley

industries

Between 1859 and 1863 events were taking place in Canada and Michigan which were to have a lasting effect on the lives of thousands of people in the middle valley of the Androscoggin River and in fact, on the peoples of the world. For, during this period, two young boys were employed as news butchers on the Grand Trunk Railroad, going through the passenger trains and hawking their wares of newspapers, magazines, candy, and guide books. One of them, Thomas Alva Edison, then fourteen years old, was to acquire world fame for his inventions and discoveries which would change the face of the earth and brighten the lives of millions. The other, Hugh J. Chisholm, who was just three years older than Edison and whose endeavors would take another path, would make his mark in a growing industry and by the use of his friend's discoveries in electricity, utilize the latent power of the great falls at Rumford, Maine.

The boys were not intimate, but were to remain life-long friends. There was a time when they were employed on different runs of the Grand Trunk, both terminating in Detroit, Chisholm on Toronto-Detroit trains and Edison on the Detroit-Port Huron route. Chisholm was fascinated by the experiments of the younger lad in his makeshift laboratory in a baggage car in the Detroit yards. Edison was impressed with the business sagacity of his older friend who was in the process of organizing with a younger brother, the firm of Chisholm Brothers. It would soon acquire the franchise for the sale of newspapers, candy, and sandwiches on more and more trains of the Grand Trunk. It is thought that Chisholm even discussed young Edison's joining forces with the Chisholm brothers, but if true the proposition apparently did not appeal to Tom Edison for he was too much of a dreamer to settle in such a mundane business. Hugh Chisholm, however, knew where he was going, and although he had started work at thirteen with nothing but a grammar school education he had invested his savings in a Toronto commercial night school course and read widely. It was said many years later by a professor at Bowdoin College that he was astonished that Hugh J. Chisholm, a cultured man and one of the most well-read, was devoid of formal education. It is possible that it was his interest in the printed word which led to his becoming a dominant figure in the production of the paper those words were printed upon.

In 1872 Chisholm Brothers had become a prosperous concern with the franchise for "news butchering" on the entire Grand Trunk System, and in addition had acquired a printing plant for publishing Railway Guide Books and tourist literature. However, the country served by the railway south of the Canadian border and the opportunities offered there beckoned Hugh Chisholm, so at thirty years of age he divided up his territory with his brother who retained the Canadian business.

Hugh Chisholm moved to Portland, Maine, the southern terminus of the Grand Trunk system and of his publishing enterprise, became a naturalized citizen of the United States and started his career as a financier and industrialist. His first venture into the wood pulp field was not in paper but in wood fibre-ware when he acquired a patent on an invention for the process and organized the Somerset Fibre Company at Fairfield, Maine, on the Kennebec. This was a successful venture but the plant was destroyed by fire soon after its start. It was rebuilt but the slow start was probably the reason for the delay in the Androscoggin enterprises in which Chisholm became involved later. Meantime Chisholm became fascinated by the unde-veloped area of the Androscoggin Valley which had been bypassed by the railroad, and in fact he had begun acquiring woodlands above Livermore. Then in 1881 he organized the Umbagog Paper Company at Livermore Falls, to manufacture paper from groundwood with the soda process. He was finally in the area where he was to direct great enterprises for thirty years.

In the winter of 1882 Chisholm made a trip to Bethel from Portland by rail, then hired a sled and drove to Rumford where he saw the great falls of the Androscoggin and visioned something of the transforma-tion of the wild waterway into a power generating giant, and the sleepy rural village of eight hundred into a bustling city surrounding a huge industrial complex. The dream was no idle one, for shortly afterwards he began quietly to acquire the land around the falls and to continue his acquisition of woodlands above the river and extending northwest almost to the New Hampshire border at Lake Umbagog and eventually touching the great woodland holdings of the Berlin Mills company. This was his first view of what he later called his second home, for Chisholm, like W. W. Brown, of the upper valley, never lived in Rumford but remained a resident of Portland until his death.

The Rumford plans were not Chisholm's sole interest during these early years, however, but remained a private side enterprise while he was engaged in operating Umbagog Paper Company in Livermore. In 1887 with two associates, A. N. Burbank and W. A. Russell of Portland, he organized the Otis Falls Paper Company at Livermore and began the manufacture of sulfite papers at that point. This operation was to last until 1966, owned then by International Paper Company.

During the ten years following, while mainly engaged in the operation of the Otis Mill, Chisholm was also employed in his long-range plans for the development in Rumford. Knowing that the three requisites for a successful integrated paper concern were woodlands for raw materials, power for manufacturing, and transportation for marketing the product, he directed his efforts toward his acquisition of woodlands and took two giant steps toward filling the other two needs. In 1890 he formed the Rumford Falls Power Company, of which he was the largest stockholder and dams were erected to divert the water through a system of canals for generating water power. He then purchased controlling stock in the near-bankrupt Rumford Falls and Buckfield Railway Company which had reached only within seven-

Rumford Falls Power Dam and Power Plant in 1899 . . .
considerably expanded since 1891 when the photo
shown on page 104 was taken.

teen miles of Rumford, at Gilbertville in Canton. The refinanced railroad completed the line to Rumford and connected with both the Grand Trunk and the Maine Central Railroad. He also bought out the partially completed Rumford Falls and Rangeley Lakes Railroad which followed the Ellis River to Bemis, thus insuring forever rail haulage of pulpwood from the great forests to Rumford. Both rail lines were later leased to the Maine Central Railroad and eventually sold to the system. Chisholm was not interested in operating railroads but was interested in someone's doing so. Thus, by 1899 he had the three essentials for his dream fulfillment. Oxford Paper Company was born and the first unit built of what was to become one of the largest integrated mills in the world.

This remarkable man, Hugh J. Chisholm, in his operation of the Otis Mill* in Livermore, had become convinced that the marketing of newsprint, which this mill was primarily producing, would be much more effective if there was some cooperation among the New England producers who were manufacturing practically all of that product used in the United States. These mills had been springing up all over New England and upper New York State and as a consequence the price of newsprint was chaotically unstable. Chisholm and his associates, Burbank and Russell, began to discuss the problem with the other newsprint manufacturers with the result in 1898 of the formation of the International Paper Company, a merger of twenty newsprint mills in Maine, New Hampshire, Vermont, Massachusetts, and upper New York State. The Glen Mill was in Berlin, New Hampshire, and the Otis Mill at Livermore Falls, Maine. The guiding light in the enormous sales job which created this combination was Hugh J. Chisholm and the first President of International Paper Company was A. N. Burbank, his associate at Otis. Both Chisholm and Russell were vice presidents of the new corporation and Russell succeeded Burbank as president after less than a year and Chisholm became the third president a few months later, to remain in that position until 1907 when he served for two years as chairman of the board.

The effect of all of these corporate maneuvers on the valley of the Androscoggin and its people was far reaching. In Livermore Falls, where the Otis and Umbagog Mills were located, there was a steady

*Oxford Paper Company never went into newsprint production and consequently was not involved in the formation of International Paper Company. Chisholm retained almost total ownership of Oxford separate and distinct from his interest in International Paper Company.

growth of permanent population as the mills were built and wood brought in from the woodlands above the town. It was followed by a stabilization period which actually has lasted to this day. The old type of woodsman in this area had passed with the Bangor tigers and the woods labor force here had pretty well steadied down to a permanent one in the last decade of the century. A conglomeration of mixed national origins had filtered into the area for the actual operation of the pulp and paper machines, and even the discontinuance of the "old" mill, the Umbagog, whose process of soda pulp had been superseded by the sulfite process at Otis, made little difference in the town population. There was still a slight swell in activity when the spring log drives came down but it was nothing like the old days when long logs were coming through from way upriver. Now it was simply a question of bringing enough pulpwood down for the requirements of a comparatively small mill. The personnel required was not great, and those who did come down on the drive were attracted by the fleshpots of Lewiston and did not linger long in little Livermore Falls.

In Rumford the effect of Chisholm's operations was far different and the transformation of the little rural town of eight or nine hundred in 1890 by tenfold in so short a period of time created all of the complications of a gold strike boom town. Hundreds of construction workers on the railroad, the power plant, and later the Oxford Paper Mill, poured into town. The townspeople were almost entirely unprepared for the influx, for while they were aware of the possibility of some development due to Chisholm's property purchases, they were pessimistic, for they had been subjected to many disappointments previously. They had seen the mild boom of lumbering in the fifties, and as logging had moved West they had seen the gradual stagnation of trade when merchants closed shop and went out of business, or moved upriver to the New Hampshire towns. As a consequence few of the old residents really profited greatly from the boom, and there was considerable resentment at the changes, particularly among the older residents, and there were not many youngsters left. They resented the fact that newcomers were opening stores and doing most of the business, that their longtime quiet streets were crowded with brawling laborers in the evenings, and what had become one of the driest towns in dry Maine now had as many "blind tigers" as dissolute Lewiston which the good church people of the old town of Rumford considered a veritable Gomorrah. Then too, they resented the incursion of "foreigners" into their Yankee community, for the rail workers were a mixture of Italian, Irish, Polish, and German immigrants, with a scattering of French-Canadians. The latter really came in with the completion of the Oxford Paper plant and by the first decade of the twentieth century their proportion of population was about the same as that of Lewiston, or seventy percent. The railroad workers and the construction men employed on the power plant, mill and dam building generally did not remain as permanent settlers but the French-Canadians did. They came from Lewiston where the labor market was saturated at the turn of the century, and from the Kennebec towns of Waterville and Augusta, where the same situation existed in the textile business. Since the economy of lower Quebec had improved very little, certainly not enough to take care of the prolific French families, many came directly from Quebec because they had relatives in the States who were making good wages in industry.

W. P. Lapham, writing in 1889 just before these developments took place, indicated lucidly what the thinking was concerning the future of the town when he described rather wistfully the Falls at Rumford: "They are, unrivalled in New England for purposes of propelling machinery and would give employment to hundreds of operators of looms and spinning machines, of both sexes . . . There is no reason why a Manchester, a Lowell or a Lewiston, should not spring up around Rumford at no distant day." He went on to say that "railway facilities will be needed, however, and there seems no bright prospect of this being accomplished soon." Lapham did know at that time of the purchase of nine-hundred acres of land near the Falls by Chisholm and Charles D. Brown, of Portland but he thought it was speculative, and for possible textile development. Chisholm's plans had been kept to himself rather securely and this too was resented by many of the older residents. It did not matter, however, for the old families were so far in the minority that it did not affect the booming development.

The dawn of the twentieth century marked the culmination of two phases of the transition of the Androscoggin River. With the dams and industrial developments at Berlin, Rumford, and Livermore, economic development had become stabilized, and the pollution of the stream from Berlin to Lewiston had begun in earnest. True, it took another forty years to bring it to its shameful worst, but rarely after the turn of the century did salmon or shad dare the entrance at Merrymeeting Bay. Whether just the textile waste and raw sewage from Lewiston and Auburn could have produced the condition is doubtful, but

"The Island" at Rumford, Maine contains its own
business area (foreground), and Oxford Paper
Company's research and development center and
pulp mill.

certainly the combination of sulfite waste liquors from Berlin, Rumford, and Livermore and their added sewage, made inevitable the eventual contamination.

By 1911 the town of Rumford was humming with activity due to the operation of the Oxford Paper Company and somehow, it is not clear how, the word of the thriving little community came to Stephen Muskie, an itinerant tailor who had emigrated from Poland. He had assumed the name Muskie upon his arrival at Ellis Island for he thought his real name, Marciszewski, would be detrimental to his progress in the new country. It was possible that the clerk who made the entry in his original papers decided that the simpler spelling of what he understood the young man to say would suit both his own convenience and the immigrant's ability to get along in the new country. Whatever the reason, it suited Stephen, and forever after he and his family used this spelling. Stephen Muskie went from New York to Buffalo where he was employed as a tailor and apparently was a very good one. He was married in the spring of 1911 and two days later he and his bride moved to the new little industrial town of Rumford, Maine.

His bride, the beautiful eighteen-year-old daughter of Polish emigrants whom he had met through Polish friends in Buffalo, was Josephine Czarnecki, whose parents had not Americanized the spelling of their name. She, however, was happy with the new simplified spelling of her husband's name. Six children were born in the next decade and the second child, the older of two boys, was born in 1914 and named Edmund Sixtus Muskie. The Sixtus was father Stephen's selection, for as a devout Catholic and avid reader of religious history, he had always admired Pope Sixtus IV for whom the Sistine Chapel had been built. With such a heavy middle name, it is not surprising that he was a serious youngster who was more interested in books than in violent athletics. One of his schoolmates said he had always thought Ed would be a priest. However, he was a real boy with interest in the things that all boys enjoy which included fishing and sitting by the bank of a beautiful river. By this time, in 1928 when he was fourteen, the river was off limits for swimming except for surreptitious dips by the youngsters when adults were not looking. The beautiful Androscoggin was rapidly becoming polluted. What the influence on a sensitive boy was at that stage is guess work, but his activities later as Governor of Maine, then Senator from Maine, and finally Chairman of the Senate Sub-Committee on Water Pollution would indicate that the Androscoggin of his boyhood had great bearing on his efforts for passage of the federal reclamation legislation of the sixties, of which he was the driving force.

4

the Depths . . . the Hope

CHAPTER 17

the

period of

unhampered pollution

1900-1941

During the latter part of Lyndon B. Johnson's first term a rather widespread campaign against the pollution of our rivers began. News stories with editorial comment appeared and perhaps the strongest message was transmitted through Bill Mauldin's 1964 cartoon of the pathetic little boy with a fishing rod staring at a sick and fetid trickling stream with sewage and industrial waste pouring in from above. On a rotting tree stump was a sign with two death heads and this warning: "Danger—pollution—no swimming—no fishing."

In February, 1966, the President proposed the legislation which would enable the industries, states, and municipalities to start (with ample federal funds to help) a gigantic campaign to reclaim our streams to their full usefulness and recreational value. The cartoon was printed over and over as the wave of public interest gathered momentum. It is to be hoped it will be repeated from time to time to remind us that this aim must be accomplished.

The Androscoggin River of Maine and New Hampshire is a fine example of what can be accomplished by the cooperation of industry and public officials. Her comeback started not in the 1960's under the aegis of the administration of John F. Kennedy or Lyndon B. Johnson, but in 1941, spurred on by the outcry of an aroused public at the appalling odor which was rising from their shamefully polluted river and the peeling paint from houses located as far as a mile away from the stream itself.

The contamination of the Androscoggin River began long before the twentieth century with the first logging on the stream and gathered momentum as millions of logs spewing bark and resinous sap discolored the water and deposited solids on the bottom. Then came the sawmills, and more and more sawdust and bark-covered slabs were dumped into the convenient river. You never saw an old sawdust pile near the river as you did at inland sawmill sites. The mill operators said that it should go into the river due to the constant fire danger. How could a little sawdust affect a tremendous flow of water like that?

Mills blossomed all up and down the valley. Domestic and human wastes were added also when the larger towns began to install sewage systems with outlets that emptied into the river. There was no thought of doing any harm to the river for there was always water rushing down to the sea. At first they were right, for the flow was able to take care of the limited amount of waste in the early days. There has been a common theory that a river will repurify itself in a mile or two, certainly in ten, and unfortunately that belief has continued over the years among laymen. This fundamental misbelief is responsible for the present state of our streams.

It is quite true that with a small amount of solids or even chemicals, the dilution of x number of gallons of water will reduce the contamination to the vanishing point, and add to this dilution the beneficial effects of aeration which take place on fast streams, at cascades, and waterfalls, and you can see where the theory originated.

In the last half of the nineteenth century there was a change in the minor contamination which had gone practically unnoticed for a hundred years, and the big textile development in Lewiston was the first offender. Thousands of gallons of dye wastes, more of bleach effluent, and tons of wool and cotton fibre particles as well as strong chemical wastes from the washings of raw wool were added to the ever

Two nearby Brown Company mills on the New
Hampshire loop of the Androscoggin; the Cascade
Mill at Gorham (top) blends with the early morning
mist, and the Berlin Mills dominate the east side of the
river.

increasing flow of sewage. It is probable that there were few complaints except from the salmon fishermen in the valley, for by the 1880's the contamination plus the erection of dams had practically stopped the great fish from migrating up to the spawning places in the tributaries.

The real villain of the cast now made his entrance with the shifting of paper mills to the sulfite process of pulping. Again there can be little blame placed on the industrialists for they also were laboring under the conviction that rivers repurify themselves and they could have no idea that their waste sulfite liquors would grow into such tremendous tonnage over the next few years. Neither did they realize that the effect of their waste could have such damaging results to the river by destroying the dissolved oxygen content of the water. Their chemists might possibly have prophesied the effect if their research had run that way, but after all, they were only charged with the responsibility of creating a cheaper and more efficient method of extracting and discharging the unwanted substances from wood for papermaking.

By 1905 all of the actors concerned with the eventual contamination of the river were on stage: logging and storage of pulpwood above Berlin, New Hampshire, sulfite waste and paper solids pouring into the river from Berlin Mills Company at Berlin and Gorham, plus the effluent from the Glen Mill of International Paper Company, and town sewage from Berlin, Gorham, and Bethel, downriver in Maine. At Rumford there were tons of sulfite waste liquors and residue from the Oxford Paper Company and International Paper Company, plus raw sewage from Rumford, Mexico, and Dixfield, and wood waste from all. Both mills at Rumford were driving the river with pulpwood as well as the tributary Swift River. Going on downriver at Livermore Falls, the International Paper Company contributed its share of sulfite liquor plus raw sewage from Livermore and Jay. Further down Lewiston and Auburn added sewage from their fifty thousand residents, plus the highly colored waste from the textile mills. Beyond, Lisbon Falls with its woolen mill and Pejepscot and its paper mill, Brunswick, where it all started with the first sawmill in the 18th century, now added nothing but textile waste and its own sewage when the mill was running. However, there was little reason to be concerned with additions at Brunswick, for the river was thoroughly polluted by the time it reached the Topsham Narrows.

The process continued all through the ups and downs of the economy with the amount of pollution varying slightly with the operation of the mills. It receded somewhat in industrial waste during slack periods and advanced sharply during boom eras, such as the World War I period when the textile and paper manufacturers were running full shifts seven days a week. However, there were too few slack times of industrial effluent and as the population of the towns steadily increased so did their domestic waste.

The cooperation in the flood control and management of the Androscoggin water levels of the major industries on the river actually started back in 1908-1909 and continued with varying success until the 1940's when it became necessary for a concerted effort to be made for the reclaiming of the polluted water. About 1908 it was realized that, while the Union Water Power Company fairly well controlled the flow from the Rangeley Lakes sources, the Magalloway River and its vast watershed west of the lakes was uncontrolled. Each spring a gigantic mass of freshet-driven water joined the outlet of Umbagog and the Errol Dam was unable to cope with the situation. The Union Water Power Company officials made contact with the authorities at Berlin Mill Company, International Paper Company, and the Oxford Paper Company and convinced them of the feasibility of a joint enterprise to build a big storage dam at Aziscohos Falls of the Magalloway River to create an artificial lake nearly twenty miles in length which would, in effect, complete the control of the flow of the entire river. This was done, and the dam built and finished in 1911 with all four companies jointly owning the completed facility which is known as The Androscoggin Reservoir Company. With The Union Water Power Company it jointly controls, through a common agent, the river's flow from the Canadian border to Merrymeeting Bay.

In 1926-1927 the new Central Maine Power Company's Gulf Island power dam just above Lewiston increased the pollution further. This was the last dam to be built on the river and made a total of twenty-one between the sources at the Canadian border and the sea. The value of the dams in controlling the water flow is unquestioned and the elimination of most flood damage has been accomplished, but there are several factors which cause a marked increase in pollution.

First, the dams eliminate to a great extent the aerating function of the cascades and falls because water no longer rushes down over rocky obstructions and bounces spray into the air to pick up oxygen. The second serious effect on pollution control is the considerable increase in water retention time which the scientists tell us is very bad if the dissolved oxygen content is low. This dissolved oxygen content is the main factor in the repurifying process and in the retaining of vegetation on the stream bottom. Without it the vegetation which is an absolute necessity for fish life is lost. The third serious effect on pollution control caused by the presence of dams is the increase in river temperature resulting from the greater area of water exposed for longer periods of time to the heat of the summer sun.

None of these facts were known by many people in the Androscoggin Valley or even suspected except by a few thoughtful Maine scientists who were gravely concerned, but whose voices were unheard or certainly unheeded. In 1930 the managements of several pulp mills in Maine evidenced their awareness of the need for information on the condition of all five of the industrial rivers in Maine, including the Androscoggin, and agreed to finance river surveys. These were carried out under the supervision of Dr. C. L. Walker of Cornell University. The Androscoggin survey was made from July to October 1930 and a report submitted to the governor and council in March, 1931. The results showed that the river was not seriously polluted at that time, but did indicate that improvement in the situation would require the joint efforts of both Maine and New Hampshire "should the load of the stream be materially increased, or the river flow be decreased relative to the volume of waste now entering it." This may have meant something to scientists but apparently did not to the governor nor the council. It is possible that the Walker report showed a slight decline in tonnage of waste in that year, for after the market crash of October 29, 1929, the production of pulp and textiles had dropped to the lowest point in the century. The Androscoggin plants were affected as much as others in the country.

The paper companies had their troubles too. Brown Company in Berlin, New Hampshire (the name was changed in World War I from Berlin Mills Company due to the anti-German hysteria), had been spread too thinly in attempting too soon to pioneer in diversification and total integration of plant processes, and was in financial difficulties. The Brown management had been pouring their profits, which were large in the boom years, into a chloroform plant in 1909, a sulfite chloride plant in 1917, a carbon tetrachloride process in 1918, a liquid chlorine plant in 1921, and a calcium arsenate facility in 1924. In addition they had been producing food products by using hydrogen for catalyzing vegetable oils. This involved them in an expensive law suit which went to the Supreme Court and which they won, but it did them little good as the supply of raw vegetable oils was controlled by the oil

unhampered pollution / 143

people who were in litigation with them. The result was that the Brown family, who had built the business with ingenuity and farsighted effectiveness, lost their control and eventually their interest in the corporation. This started a series of changes in ownership, mostly absentee, and management, which seriously hampered its progress during the next fifteen years.

International Paper Company fared much better. It retrenched by closing a number of mills which had obsolete equipment. Two of the mills eliminated were on the Androscoggin: the Glen Mill at Berlin and their mill at Rumford. Oxford Paper Company fared the best of all and it was probably due to the fact that the unbroken line of management of the Chisholms still followed the senior Chisholm's rules of conservative but progressive management. The textile business in the Lewiston area suffered two-fold during the depression and even afterward, for like all New England textiles, the movement was to the South, with its modern plants and lower labor costs. It was inevitable that with the general business depression, the effects on labor were almost cataclysmic. Nevertheless, during the later 1930's the economy of the valley began to recover slowly and by 1938 the demand for war materials had pulled both industries back to the profit side of the ledger. Textiles in the remaining Lewiston mills had settled down to highly specialized cloths and synthetics, and the pulp and paper business was booming with packaging materials for shipments to the war zone.

In the spring of 1936, following a tremendous snowfall, disaster struck northern New England when the three elements which invariably cause floods were joined in spectacular fashion. First, there was the heavy snow cover in January and February which was unusually high in water content, next, in March, came a sudden thaw, then rain and more rain, resulting in such masses of water that the overflow at all dams was counted in feet, not inches, and there was an excess of flowage in millions of gallons per second seeking outlets to sea level. All Maine and New Hampshire streams were affected but the Androscoggin probably most of all, for its narrow valley in the seventy-odd miles above Livermore acted as a high pressure pump forcing water into a fire main. The Androscoggin was subjected to two separate and distinct surges. First, ice came down in great floating hulks and battered the dams and bridges, taking some of the latter and weakening others. After a hiatus of a couple of days, more rain fell and the river level, which had not had time enough to recede, was swelled anew and the resulting onrush of mad water finished the already weakened riverside structures and bridges. It was in the second flushing that the lower bridge from Auburn to Lewiston went out, though the first surge had taken the Brunswick-Topsham span as well as others all up the river. The damage ran into the millions though most of the dams came through with minor damage to flood gates and baffles. Many of the residents sighed after viewing the damage, and then remarked that perhaps it did do some good because the old river certainly did need a thorough flushing out of its bottom. No doubt they were right and it may have done some good, but the contamination had gone too far and industry was interrupted only a few days in its dumping of tons of waste liquors.

Another survey was made by private interests in 1940, this time by the well known Boston engineering firm of Metcalf and Eddy for the Central Maine Power Company, the owners of the Gulf Island Power Dam. Its report must have been quite damning for it was never published nor were the results made public. By this time the sulfite pulp production had reached its apex with nearly 6,000 *tons* of oxygen-devouring waste liquors pouring into the river each week and untold tons of insoluble solids building up a coating on the river bottom which effectively destroyed all life-giving vegetation.

Thus New Year's day, 1941, ushered in a year which not only would plunge the country into World War II, but would bring to a climax the terrible contamination of one of America's loveliest rivers. The winter of '41 began with an unusually scanty snowfall. It was an open winter and no good word can be found for an "open winter" among the old time residents who say that "it ain't healthy" and they are certainly right as to the health of an already polluted stream.

Snowfall was light and in addition there were no less than three winter thaws which took off the scarce snow unseasonably early. When spring came, by the calendar, there was no freshet, no great mass of water rushing down to the sea. The result was that the river was at the lowest level it had been for many a season. Now came the culminating factor, an unusually hot June and July with little rain. From a faint whiff of hydrogen sulfite which rose from the river in May, the appalling stench of rotten eggs became progressively worse all up and down the river, and reached its climax in the most heavily populated section of Lewiston and Auburn, where roughly sixty thousand indignantly aroused citizens became vocally and politically vehement. It was a community disaster which was not only the topic of all conversation, but caused the slowdown of industry and business in general. Retail stores were deserted and some suffered physically from the effluvia. Jewelers for example, nearly went berserk keeping their stocks of silverware saleable because the sulfite-laden air turned silver and other metals black overnight. If you were driving from Augusta to Lewiston you began to smell it at North Monmouth, twenty miles from the city, and it increased in intensity as the road approached the river. Houses painted white turned black and blistered in great ugly patches, and by the time you had reached the city limits, you had to put up your car windows despite the heat and try not to breathe through your nose. It was revolting, and the exodus of families who could afford it became a locust-like invasion of the seashore and the mountain and lakeside camps, provided they were located far from the foul river. The wage earners must of necessity remain and their outcries reached such a volume that the matter was brought before the newly created Maine Sanitary Water Board. Late in August that body employed the same firm of Metcalf and Eddy of Boston to conduct a survey of the river and to recommend remedial measures. Thus, out of the despair and suffering of the populace was born the infant movement to recover the river.

CHAPTER 18

the

recovery years

1941-1975

For the industries dotting the 138 mile stretch of the Androscoggin below Berlin, New Hampshire, the odor calamity of 1941 posed obvious and immediate problems. Everyone within reach of the river who breathed regularly knew the source of the noxious pollution that nauseated the senses, peeled the paint from the walls, and drove residents in affected areas out of town. The public outcry was vehement and political pressure for corrective action began to rattle the lid of the corporate pot.

For corporate and plant management the situation was made doubly difficult by the unhappy timing of the odor outbreak, the effect of which coincided with a rising wartime demand for the industrial goods of the valley. This unprecedented surge of profitable business, coming after the long and dreary depression and post depression years when the very existence of valley industry was in peril, required full production, pollution or no pollution. The economic well-being of much of the valley and its people, as well as corporate profit, was riding on it.

The situation deteriorated further in February of 1942 when Metcalf and Eddy presented a summary of their field tests to the Maine Sanitary Water Board. Their report stated that ninety-six percent of the Androscoggin's pollution could be traced to industrial wastes; ninety-two percent of it from pulp and paper mills, and only a minor share from textile wastes. The pulp and paper industry was clearly identified as the villain and its deeply concerned managements learned that seventy-seven percent of their collective contribution stemmed from sulfite waste liquor, an inevitable by-product of the sulfite pulping process then in use.

The consulting firm's immediate recommendation was that pulp and paper manufacturers be persuaded, or forced if need be, to segregate their sulfite wastes, impound them in storage lagoons during summer months, and discharge them into the river in the fall only when flows and water temperature permitted. This practical recommendation was admittedly a stopgap measure, and was obviously the only solution the consultants could offer. It would enable the industry to continue to produce by its existing processes and would certainly reduce the odor problem, but it promised no permanent cure for the ailing Androscoggin.

Industry had recognized the seriousness of the pollution problem and the need to cure it for its own and the public's good well before the odor catastrophe occurred. Informal consultations during the late 1930's among the managements and technical staffs of Brown, Oxford, International Paper, and outside experts finally led to the formation of the Androscoggin River Technical Committee in 1942. Though its early activities were primarily investigative and exploratory, it was destined to play a major role in the eventual rehabilitation of the river, and events immediately following the Metcalf and Eddy report provided the impetus.

In May of 1942 the Attorney General of Maine submitted to the Maine Supreme Judicial Court in Equity an "information" which cited discharge of sulfite waste liquor from the mills of Brown, Oxford, and International Paper as the cause of recurrent obnoxious odors from the river. The Court promptly ordered the companies to show cause for not being enjoined from such action. The ultimate result was a series of agreements drawn in December, 1942, January, 1944, December,

1947, and December, 1948, setting progressively reduced weekly limits on combined waste discharge from the mills. The 1948 agreement gave the authority to set weekly quotas to the Administrator of the Androscoggin River, River Master Walter A. Lawrance. The cleanup of the Androscoggin had begun to come full circle.

Dr. Lawrance, then head of the Chemistry Department of Bates College in Lewiston and acknowledged technical expert on water management in general and Androscoggin pollution in particular, had become a consulting member of the Technical Committee in 1943. With his appointment as administrator or River Master in 1947 and court-assigned responsibility for control in 1948, the essential cleanup of the river began to take on shades of reality. Here was a man who understood the technical complexities of both pollution abatement and pulp mill processing, recognized the impossibility of instant compliance by the mill owners, yet was totally dedicated to the premise that the Androscoggin should, and could, be cleaned up without destroying the economy of the valley.

His was the role of catalyst in the struggle for controlling pollution of the river during a period in which both mill owners and the state water boards of Maine and New Hampshire were aware of the then shaky legal authority with which he was empowered. That he made it work, avoiding open confrontation of these two factions during a difficult transitional period, is a tribute to both his personal effectiveness and the sincerity of both parties in seeking a practical solution.

Admittedly, repairing the ravages of more than a half century of pollution is slow and costly work. Nevertheless the record of progress in cleaning up industrial pollution on the Androscoggin since the 1940's has been impressive. In his Administrator's Progress Report of March 15, 1967, Dr. Lawrance stated as outstanding accomplishments the elimination of serious odor nuisance, the complete and permanent elimination of the sulfite pulping process at Berlin, New Hampshire, and Rumford and Jay, Maine (Chisholm and Livermore Falls), and appreciable reduction in discharge of suspended solids and process water.

During this twenty-five year period a great deal of money was invested in trying to save the sulfite process by building lagoons and installing treatment equipment which would minimize the pollution hazard of sulfite wastes. In the main it was a costly and unsatisfactory solution. The turning point was industry management's realization that a switch from the sulfite to the kraft pulping process was their only economic answer. With their commitment to invest the huge sums required for process conversion the promise of the Androscoggin's rehabilitation became a reality.

The closing of the sulfite mills on the river is the factual record of this progress. In 1943 Brown's Cascade mill was closed, in 1949 Oxford Paper's Oxford Division mill was shut down, and in 1961 its Island Division closed its doors. By 1965, with the closing of the last Brown Company sulfite mill on the river, only International Paper Company's sulfite operation at Livermore Falls remained. When, in 1966, International Paper opened its big new $54 million kraft mill at Jay, this last vestige of the sulfite days closed its doors. For the first time since 1892, when the Burgess mill at Berlin, New Hampshire, went on stream, the Androscoggin was free of its old enemy, sulfite liquor.

It had been a long, difficult, and costly road not without its bruises and temporary setbacks. For instance, the opening of International Paper Company's big Kraft mill at Jay in 1966 was temporarily a mixed blessing for the improving but still turgid waters of the Androscoggin. It enabled the company to shut down its pulping operations at its Livermore Falls plant permanently and stop forever the threat of its sulfite waste products. However, it immediately posed another if lesser problem in the disposal of millions of gallons per day of process waste at Jay. True, waste water from Jay's kraft process papermaking operations had only a fraction of the pollution impact of potent sulfite waste liquors, but nonetheless added temporarily to the further pollution of the lower river.

This problem too has been dealt with through infusions of capital investment and technology. Primary treatment facilities installed in 1968-1969 were the first step and a secondary treatment plant completed in 1973 removes over eighty-five percent of pollutants from the mill's total waste flow, a good record in any ecological league.

International Paper Company's investment in capital improvements did not stop with the original Androscoggin Mill. Additions and equipment improvements, including the secondary treatment facilities, had reached over $100 million by the end of 1973. In the spring of 1974 plans for an enormous addition to the mill with two additional paper machines were announced. Approval was sought from the Environmental Protection Agency and state authorities, with a budgeted estimate of some $140 million, which it was said was the largest individual investment the company had ever made.

The effects of the consummation of these new International Paper Company plans on the economy of the area around Livermore Falls cannot be estimated. They certainly will be considerable and are certain to include several hundred new employees in both the production and woods operations.

The rehabilitation of the Androscoggin following the explosion of public opinion in 1941 is a classic example of what it takes to bring a river basin back from the edge of disaster. Public awareness of need, often emotionally arrived at as in the case of the odor problems of 1941, usually provides the trigger. Nevertheless the accomplishment calls for recognition of the common interest among all concerned parties and the ability to develop a considered and rational approach to an ultimate solution which neither wrecks an economy nor destroys an enterprise. To this must be added a great deal of time, effort, and money, and all were a part of the Androscoggin cleanup.

*   *   *   *

Interestingly enough, the rehabilitation of the Androscoggin triggered by the odor crisis of 1941 was somewhat ahead of its time, at least in terms of the ecological frenzy which gathered momentum nationally during the 1960's. One day the sociologists, political scientists, and economists will unravel the confused threads of that dynamic decade and put together a recognizable pattern of cause and effect. Complex and confusing, it was nonetheless clearly the decade of revolt and change. Revolt of youth, minorities, and the consumer. Revolt against an ill-conceived and agonizingly unpopular war. Revolt against man's careless and often selfish depletion and befoulment of the earth's natural resources. It was a decade in which the common man rose up to challenge a host of established patterns and mores, and "save our environment" was one of his early battle cries.

It is, of course, axiomatic of revolt that its just target is often neither fully understood nor clearly defined, and the revolutionist, however noble his cause, is often prone to sink his axe with unreasoned abandon into the most conveniently available skull. For the concerned, sincere, and completely well-intentioned citizen-soldier of the ecological movement of the sixties, industry was a highly visible target. Did it not pollute? It did, and there were credible statistics to prove it. Did it care? There was not much evidence to show it. Had it done anything about it? Not much, in his view, despite the sudden spate of corporate communication to the contrary.

It is not particularly strange that he showed so little concern for his own role as a polluter. Very few good citizen-soldiers take the trouble to find out, and where would they, that each contributes his hundred gallons per day to the local sewer, not to mention a like contribution from his wife and each of the children. After all, is that not a municipal job? Who wants to point a finger at himself or raise taxes? In his defense is the inescapable fact that in the frenetic noise of a burgeoning crusade the popular half-truths outweigh the facts and simplistic answers are the order of the day. Who was to put into fair perspective all the complexities of public vs private responsibility for pollution and its related economic and technical questions when even the experts disagreed?

Well informed or not as to causes, problems, or solutions, the crusade gained momentum and the pressure of its noise began to register on the eardrums of those inhabiting the federal establishment along the Potomac. Though government can rarely be accused of being exquisitely sensitive and responsive to public needs and demands, it does know a good, loud, noise when it hears one espousing a popular cause. Suddenly, in the mid-sixties, popular concern for the environment was "in," ecology was a household word and yet another cycle in the periodic game of enforcing pollution control was on the upturn in Washington.

Just how much real effect all this had on the Androscoggin program already well underway would be difficult to determine. In one view it could be concluded that very little direct benefit and even less money filtered up through the smog of hearings, congressional action, executive delay, administrative musical chairs, and the pullings and haulings between federal and state agencies which took place during the period. On the other hand, federal legislation was passed which affected both industrial and municipal pollution in all the states, even Maine and New Hampshire, and presumably a reasonable share of federally authorized funds trickled into the Androscoggin watershed municipal projects, however haltingly.

During this period a broad spectrum of the federal establishment was getting the message from the grass roots and flexing its muscles to leap aboard the antipollution bandwagon. Congress in particular was feeling the heat in terms of much-needed legislation, for its action in this area during the 1950's and early 1960's had, at best, been sporadic. Suddenly it was a time for action and the highly visible key figures in the limelight were Senator Edmund Muskie (D) of Maine, Chairman of the Senate Sub-Committee on Air and Water Pollution, and Congressman John Blatnick (D) of Minnesota, then Chairman of the House Public Works Rivers and Harbors Sub-Committee. Both were highly knowledgeable with impressive records of familiarity with both pollution and polluters.

The craggy, homespun Senator from Maine gained considerable stature during the late sixties as a supporter of the environmental new look, a luster he carried with him into the painful presidential primaries of 1971 and still holds today. The Minnesota Congressman on the other hand, tagged in the fifties as the "Father of the Water Pollution Control Movement" by virtue of legislation he introduced during that period, lost both his title and his environmental charisma in the eyes of conservationists during the exploding sixties. Whether or not Mr. Blatnick did, as accused, become a foot-dragger and take the lead in watering down industrial pollution legislation is of less importance than the fact that progress was made in Congress. The hearings were interminable, the noise of hammering out compromise language in joint sessions was deafening, and some of the provisions voted into law were less than realistic.

The Water Quality Act of 1965 was the tangible result of the hammering and much, undeniably, was lost on the anvil of joint session compromise. It did, however, put the wheels in motion to achieve a new and better set of water quality standards and added a few new sorely needed teeth to enforcement. It also put squarely before Congress the facts of life about funding. This cleaning up of America was going to be an expensive business though just how costly was not immediately apparent.

The gap in allegedly expert estimates of how much it would take to do the job has varied between $8 and $37 billion. Regrettably, the relative gap between money appropriated by Congress between 1965 and 1970 and the aggregate expenditure authorized by the Executive has been nearly as great, a staggering shortfall of $773 million in which both the Johnson and Nixon administrations had a hand. But the confusion and political infighting on pollution control was hardly limited to the Congress and the President during this period.

In the early sixties, responsibility for administration and enforcement of such federal environmental laws as were on the books was spread widely among a number of government agencies. The Departments of Health, Education and Welfare, Interior, and Agriculture all had a part in pollution control, and the Army Corps of Engineers retained a large measure of control over navigable rivers and streams. No single agency had either the power or the machinery to deal with the complex pressures of the developing new look of environmentalism, even had the inclination to grab this highly charged wire existed. The fact that state water quality boards also had considerable authority and autonomy merely added to the general confusion.

The Division of Water Supply and Pollution Control of the U.S. Public Health Service (USPHS) was the focal point for implemental responsibility at the federal level during this period of increasing public pressure and Congressional reaction. The game of musical chairs to which it was subjected mirrored the confusion of the times. Formed in 1961 as a Division of the USPHS, the agency was transferred intact to Health, Education and Welfare in 1966. HEW's Assistant Secretary for Administration, Rufus Miles, categorized its problems and the problems of the day in quoting from the results of a management study of the ailing organization just prior to the move:

"The [program] lacks effective central direction, coordination and control; organizational and administrative discipline; the means (including staff), the procedures and the executive-level disposition to develop and exercise national-level supervision over the implementation of short and long range policies, plans and programs for the conduct of its multitudinous and far-flung water pollution control affairs."

Just five months after the move to HEW it was shifted over to Interior. In 1970 it came to rest in the federal hierarchy as a part of the newly formed Environmental Protection Agency, and with a new name, the Water Quality Office. Its staff, a very different group from that which began the work in the mid-sixties, must have hoped and prayed for a permanent home and a little stability in order to get on with the job.

People too were a part of the confusion. In the early days the USPHS group was a curious mixture of dedicated civil servants, technical experts, and political appointees. The Division's first director was ex-Congressman James Quigley, defeated Democrat from Pennsylvania appointed as an Assistant Secretary to HEW by the Kennedy Administration in 1961. His qualifications for the job when he took over in 1966 were limited to his political persuasion, and his administration proved the idiocy of political appointments in areas demanding some degree of technical expertise. His tenure lasted through a critical period, for it was 1968 before he resigned to go on to greater glory as corporate vice-president of one of the nation's most powerful wood products corporations with a decided stake in Washington's actions on pollution control.

His successor was Joe Moore of Texas, technically knowledgeable and an experienced administrator in the area of pollution problems and their cure. His appointment was hailed as brilliant by those struggling in the morass of bureaucratic confusion. Unfortunately, he had barely warmed up the seat of his new chair before the incoming Nixon administration replaced him with David Dominick, Republican, whose principal credentials were based on his service as a senatorial legislative assistant, his ardor as a campaign worker in the Nixon group, and his kinship with Senator Peter Dominick (R) of Colorado.

Whatever its leadership, when the agency landed in the lap of the EPA it brought with it many of its defects and most of its inherent bureaucratic confusion. Fortunately, it fell broadly under the guidance of William D. Ruckelshaus, Director of EPA, whose well-regarded administration did unravel some of the problems before he left this post.

EPA is confronted by an enormous task, but with the centralization of responsibility for most of the complex and interrelated facets of environmental control within one agency has come the glimmer of hope for a more orderly and practical approach at the national level. It has assumed control over all streams, not merely navigable and interstate waters, and has real enforcement clout under existing federal law in the area of industrial pollution.

Federal and state authorities are working more harmoniously in their efforts to achieve reasonable and practical solutions, and standards are more precise and better understood than at any point in history. Massive problems remain and all is not well on the environmental front, but the frenzy of the mid-sixties has brought some results.

For the Androscoggin, this all has the ring of too little and much too late. Her battle against industrial pollution was all but won when the dynamic sixties were hitting their confusing peak on the national scene.

Unlike rivers which have the misfortune to see great cities rise on their banks or to wind their way through densely populated urban sprawl, the Androscoggin cradles a mere 170,000 souls in her thousand square mile river basin. As Metcalf and Eddy's report following the foul odor outbreak of 1941 clearly stated, only four percent of the river's then sorry condition was attributable to municipal waste flows. This was a minor problem and it is hardly surprising that it received little immediate attention.

The elimination of municipal pollution inevitably poses an unhappy psychological block in the public mind, for the public is both offender and offended. Curing the problem he himself has created is going to hit John Public in the pocketbook where it hurts, and the degree of financial help available from federal and state sources is often a good barometer of his willingness to press for action.

Public pressure along the Androscoggin during the fifties and early sixties was understandably minimal. Industry was the big polluter, ecology was a relatively unknown word, and little tangible help was on the horizon from the outside world. In the main, residents of the Androscoggin basin went about their business of struggling to strengthen their economy in the postwar years, pursuing the puritan ethic, and enjoying their magnificent countryside.

At the state level an equally understandable disinterest prevailed. Not much came out of Washington that made sense or offered help and on the Androscoggin industry had already been nailed as the principal culprit and a corrective program was under way. State authorities were neither incompetent nor lax in not pushing harder. They were simply responding to the pressures of the times and had other and bigger problems to tackle.

In such action as was taken during this period, Maine took the lead. After all, 150,000 Down Easters lived in her share of the Androscoggin basin as opposed to 20,000 widely scattered New Hampshireites in the remote northeast corner of the Granite State. In terms of pollution priorities New Hampshire had the Connecticut and Merrimack to worry about. To what extent pressure from densely populated down-country areas shifted emphasis on the part of New Hampshire's huge legislature to the badly polluted Merrimack is academic. The time was not right for an all-out effort.

Nonetheless, as far back as 1955, following the passage of Public Law 660 by Congress, the water quality boards of both states began a series of surveys aimed at establishing specifications for classifying various stretches of their respective portions of the river. The results, while hardly the last word in stringency, were a vast improvement over the antediluvian classifications previously in force. It was 1966 before public hearings were held in both states and in 1967 both legislatures approved revised classifications. They were just in time to make the deadline and respond to Public Law 753, the 89th Congress' more demanding answer to public pressure at the national level.

If the new classifications were practical, the five-year deadline set for compliance by industry and municipality alike were not. Even with a sound program underway and much already accomplished, industry found it impossible in most cases to meet the prescribed deadlines. For municipalities with no planning done, limited resources of their own, and not much promise of help, the situation was hopeless. Eventually reason won out and the deadlines were extended to 1976 in Maine and 1977 in New Hampshire.

It was 1969 before a comprehensive program of municipal pollution abatement in the Androscoggin basin began to take hold, but a trip down the river today would tell a far different story from that told at any time in the immediate past. In the upper basin tributary lakes region of Maine at the little tourist town of Rangeley we find a secondary treatment plant in operation and a tertiary plant nearing completion to protect Rangeley Lake and the waters of the Androscoggin below, the latter already classified "B" or better all the way down to Berlin, New Hampshire.

At Berlin we find the city has already let the contract for the design of its secondary treatment plant with Gorham, just downriver, committed to a similar program. Taken together with Brown Company's commitment to meet all standards within the 1977 deadline, things are looking up for the New Hampshire stretch even though they lag behind Maine's timetable.

Across the Maine border and up the northbound loop of the river we find work already in progress on the interceptors which will feed the Rumford-Mexico Regional Water Pollution Control Commission's secondary treatment plant. Scheduled for completion well before the 1976 deadline at a cost of $3.6 million, it will treat all municipal waste from Rumford, Mexico, Dixfield, and West Peru as well as sanitary waste from Oxford's nearby plants. In addition Oxford's industrial treatment facilities are well along in the design stage too.

As the river swings south again we come upon another regional facility under construction, this one at Jay, a little further along toward completion. The Livermore Falls - Chisholm - Jay Sewage Disposal District will handle municipal waste from these communities as well

As it nears the sea in Maine, the Androscoggin
divides the twin cities of Auburn and Lewiston and
the Little Androscoggin (left foreground) splits the
latter.

as sanitary waste from International's Livermore Falls Otis plant. The Androscoggin Mill has treated its sanitary waste satisfactorily since the plant opened in 1965.

Moving southward we enter the Lewiston-Auburn area, the most heavily populated in the entire basin, with 70,000 inhabitants. Here, under the jurisdiction of the Lewiston-Auburn Pollution Control Authority, is a brand new secondary treatment plant completed in 1973 at a cost of $8.5 million. Big money for Maine, and small wonder the citizens of Lewiston and Auburn look upon their upriver neighbors to the northwest with a touch of resentment for their tardy action on pollution control.

Next in line on the way to the sea we come to Lisbon where construction of a secondary treatment plant to handle the combined flows of the three villages comprising the town was scheduled for fiscal 1974. Finally, we pass Brunswick and Topsham where secondary plants are already in operation.

Back up in the Little Androscoggin River Valley things are much the same, though the industrial pollution picture, involving paper mill, food, and tanning wastes, is a bit more complex. Plans for bringing industrial pollution under control are well under way, Norway's secondary treatment system is complete, and the other communities on the Little Androscoggin have plans on their drawing boards.

From the hard-core conservationist who believes in environmental purity at any price, a trip down the Androscoggin would bring a snort of outrage; the river is still polluted, secondary treatment is inadequate, progress is too slow. He might add, with some justice, caustic comment on the operations of the Water Quality Office in Washington, the continuing recurring battle with their counterparts at the state level, the inadequacy of many state standards, and the staggering shortfall and delay in promised federal funds.

The fact remains however, that the Androscoggin is a healthier river than it has been in half a century. Completion of current projects will give her a basic classification of "C" and there is a well authenticated belief that "B" or better can be accomplished for major stretches. For the 180,000 people who live in her basin this sounds a joyful note of hope.*

*Class "B" shall be accepted for recreational purposes and after adequate treatment for potable water supply; Class "C" shall be suitable for boating, fishing, and fish management but not for potable water supply or swimming unless adequately treated.

CHAPTER 19

the

future of the

Valley

From the turn of the century until the end of the Great Depression in 1940 the pollution of the Androscoggin was so gradual that the man in the street was scarcely aware of its deteriorating condition. Sportsmen had written off the use of the stream and were almost as apathetic as the general public, for the area within sixty miles of any point in the valley between Berlin, New Hampshire, and Merrymeeting Bay was replete with un-polluted ponds, lakes, and streams which afforded excellent bass, trout, and salmon fishing. To the valley inhabitants the Androscoggin, like many of the country's important waterways, had become merely a source of power, an essential of industrial processing, and a convenient carrier of man's waste to what was thought to be the unlimited capacity of the ocean.

The sudden shock of the 1941 odor calamity was the catalyst which destroyed the apathy of the citizens of the valley and marked the beginning of their consolidation of purpose to recover the river for the inhabitants. It also marked the beginning of a gradual recovery of their economy from the depths of the depression years.

In the Auburn-Lewiston area the boost to the economy caused by World War II was relatively short-lived. A mass exodus of the textile industry followed closely upon the cessation of hostilities and the late forties saw a second depression which lasted in lessening degree through the early fifties. However, business in the two big cities began to show signs of recovery with development of a trend toward diversification of industry.

Perhaps the beginning of this trend was the move to Lewiston by Geiger Brothers, the well-known calendar and novelty advertising firm, from its long established location in New Jersey. One by one other diverse industries followed, among them Pioneer Plastics Corporation whose employment level at their modern facility in Auburn had grown to roughly 600 skilled workers by 1973.

During this period Lewiston's great, gaunt, empty textile mill buildings began to fill up with small manufacturing operations, most of them, strangely enough, engaged in the shoe business which had been confined mainly to Auburn for generations. While in 1945 about eighty percent of some 8,000 Lewiston mill and manufacturing workers were employed by the textile industry, by 1971 this figure had been reduced to eighteen percent, and shoe and affiliated manufacturing plants employed fifty-nine percent of the total industrial work force of the city. At first glance it might be thought that this shift across the river was at the expense of Auburn but this is not strictly true. Auburn shoe manufacturers still employ sixty percent of that city's industrial work force, with plastics manufacturing accounting for thirteen percent, textiles five percent, and the balance scattered among metalworking, food processing, and lumber operations.

Lewiston's diversification trend continued into the 1970's and is reflected in the employment of its current industrial work force of 8,600. Of this total 5,200 are employed in shoe manufacturing and 1,450 in textile operations with the balance fairly distributed in metalworking, electronics, publishing, and food processing. Although the proportion of service personnel to population is about the same in the two cities, Lewiston can lay claim to a higher level of clerical employment by virtue of its greater concentration of retail outlets in both midtown and shopping center areas.

The intense and at times bitter rivalry which formerly existed

The Androscoggin Mill of International Paper
Company at Jay, Maine, in 1974. In right background
a portion of the big new mill's extensive pollution
control facilities.

between the two cities has been largely eliminated by a number of factors. The number of employed workers living in both cities who cross one of the bridges to work is astounding. More and more civic aspirations and efforts to accomplish them involve joint Lewiston-Auburn action. Close cooperation between the two communities is no longer the exception but the general rule. They have the same water systems, a brand new sewage disposal system of which they are jointly proud, many organizations with memberships on both sides of the river, and even a single Community Little Theatre. It is probable that only in high school athletics is the old and once bitter intercity rivalry retained.

Upriver communities, beginning with Livermore Falls, Jay, and Chisholm, have also felt the effects of this joint community attitude. With their common economic dependence on the operations of International Paper Company and the formation of their joint sewage disposal system, they have found new grounds for cooperation and their economy and community morale have shown even more improvement than that of the Lewiston-Auburn area. This trend is also very evident in the Rumford-Mexico area and extends further afield to include the rural communities of Peru and Dixfield. Oxford Paper Company's payroll directly affects the economy of the entire area and its community relations policies also carry a good deal of weight.

In New Hampshire economic improvement over the past two decades has been slower than that of the lower valley and began almost without the knowledge of the citizenry. At Berlin, Brown Company has long been the bellwether of economic stability and community well-being, and during the sixties an atmosphere of deep uncertainty was understandably prevalent. The Brown family had lost control of its mills, and a series of shifts in ownership and uncertain business conditions caused deep concern among employees and community alike. These threatening clouds have been dispersed in recent years by the clear commitment of present management not only to stay in business but to spend $25-27 million on air and water pollution control by 1977 and it has communicated its new policies well. Despite this new note of hope for the future the fact remains that Brown's employment level dropped from nearly 4,000 in 1958 to a current level of 1,700.

Over these years, some of the slack was taken up by Granite State Rubber Company, now the Granite State Division of Converse Rubber. Formed in 1946 with eight employees, this new manufacturer of canvas and rubber footwear had expanded to a work force of 400 by 1948. By 1973 the total staff numbered 1,150 in greatly expanded facilities, and though the proportion of women employed was far greater than that at Brown, the overall economic impact of this growth on Berlin was material.

Nevertheless, Berlin's population dropped approximately by 2,500 persons between 1960 and 1970 to 15,256. It is generally assumed that this directly reflects the decrease in Brown employment during the period but the figures are somewhat confusing. In the fifties and early sixties Brown was engaged in multiple woods operations with its own employees and it is probable that its total employee figure included something like a thousand woods department workers. About that time the procurement of its pulpwood was shifted over to contract jobbers with an increase in "purchased wood" and company-managed woods operations were reduced to a minimum. Though the effect on Brown's personnel statistics was material, the effect on area economy was minimal, for payrolls of jobbers and private "tree farmers" still contributed equally to the general area economy.

The problems which faced the three paper companies during the 1940's and 1950's were quite different and it happened that International Paper's were really minimal in comparison with those at Oxford and Brown. Their operations on the Androscoggin had been reduced to the small sulfite pulping plant, the Otis Mill at Livermore having closed the mills at Berlin and Rumford during the "belt tightning" era of the depression. In view of their tremendous woodland holdings in the North Country, their long-term plans contemplated vast new installations in more suitable locations than those which had been dependent upon waterpower alone.

Oxford and Brown were confronted with almost insurmountable problems in complying with the very vague though tough governmental regulations. Both had vast investments in plant and equipment and were situated on bluffs of solid granite which made new excavations difficult and expensive. Brown's plant locations, separated by several miles between the Berlin plants and that at Cascade, vastly complicated their problems. Their outlook for compliance in 1977 is a most commendable accomplishment. Both concerns deserve a great deal of credit for what they have achieved since 1972.

At the bottom of the valley, Brunswick, without the dependence on industrial operations, maintained its solid economic situation and isolation from the troubles of the upriver communities. The loss of its big yarn mill in the forties was offset by acquisition of a Naval Air Base, practically nullifying the expected drop in employment. Many workers living in Brunswick are employed steadily in the shipyard at Bath, while others commute a few miles north to the Pejepscot Paper Mill, both having maintained relatively stable employment levels.

In addition Bowdoin College provides considerable employment and rather dominates the social and intellectual atmosphere of the community. The attitude of most Brunswick citizens toward the river itself has been a philosophic acceptance of the pollution and a rather superior viewpoint that "some day" the upriver towns and industries would succeed in cleaning up the waters. That their primary sewage system preceded all others on the river by at least ten years and their secondary system by five, lends an air of justice to their somewhat unneighborly view.

*   *   *   *

To summarize the far-reaching and interrelated effects of even singular events occurring in the evolution of a river valley over the span of many centuries is, of course, impossible. Yet, within the decade just passed, the radical change of atmosphere within the basin of the Androscoggin, and the equally subtle changes in the outlook of its people are quite apparent, even to the casual observer.

The Valley of the Androscoggin is a valley of hope. Its people reflect an enthusiastic confidence in the next decade and the years to follow though it is probable that most would find it difficult to say just what transformed the hopelessness of the forties and fifties to this confidence of the present. It is certain that very few would link all the philosophical, economic, and sociological complexities that have been a part of the equation of change; yet the change is as real and as tangible as the waters of the river itself.

The river: can it have played the leading role in this transformation of attitude and viewpoint? From the beginning of time it drew to its banks those who took from it what they needed and wanted with little thought of what they gave back. In 1941 it threw back what it had been given by man, and in full measure, and the shock was catalytic and far-reaching in its ultimate effects.

It provided the opportunity for those who cared and who recognized the importance of caring to move toward its rehabilitation, however painfully and slowly. It created an atmosphere in which industry and municipality alike could realistically assess their options and act responsibly, and it led directly to renewed confidence in the stability of the valley's economy and its potential for healthy growth. Possibly most important, it led to a growing spirit of area consciousness and cooperation which one day may unite the inhabitants of the valley as never before.

BIBLIOGRAPHY

Published Volumes and Booklets

Adams, Henry, *History of the United States of America*, Vol. 5, 6, 1813-1817. New York, C. Scribner's Sons, 1891.

Allen, William, *The History of Norredgewock*. Boston, E.J. Peet, 1849.

Auburn Toll Bridge, Auburn, Maine, Androscoggin County Commissioners Records, 1823-1865.

Baldwin, Laemmi, *Water Power of Maine*. Boston, 1835.

Belknap, Jeramy, *Journal of a Tour of the White Mountains*. Massachusetts Historical Society, 1876 (Mss. of 1784).

Centennial Brochure. City of Berlin, New Hampshire, 1929.

Bishop, Morris, *Champlain, The Life of Fortitude*. New York, A.A. Knopf, 1948.

Butterfield, C.W., *History of Brules Discoveries*. Cleveland, Helmon, Taylor Co., 1898.

Carhart, Arthur, *Water or Your Life*. Philadelphia, Lippincott, 1959.

Carr, Donald E., *Death of the Sweet Waters*. New York, W.W. Norton, 1966.

Champlain, Samuel, *Voyages*. (Edited by A.N. and E.G. Bourne). New York, A.S. Barnes & Co., 1906.

Chisholm, Hugh J., Jr., *A Man and the Paper Industry*. New York, Newcomen Society, 1952.

Crawford, Lucy A., *A History of the White Mountains*. Portland, Maine, F. and A. Garrish, 1846.

Davis, Captain James, *A Relation of a Voyage to Sagadahoc* (Lambeth Mss., edited by H.O. Thayer). Portland, Maine, Gorgas Society, 1892.

Ellis, George W., and Morris, J.E., *King Phillip's War*. New York, Grafton Press, 1906.
Report on Water Pollution. New York, Federated Women's Club, 1950.
Fiske, John, *New France and New England*. Boston, Houghton, Mifflin & Co., 1902.
Goss, Thomas I., *T. Thorndyke, Attorney at Law*. Manchester, New Hampshire, 1907.
Gurnham, C.P., *Principles of Industrial Waste Treatment*. New York, John Wiley, 1955.
History of Bethel (formerly Sudberry Canada, Oxford County, Maine). Augusta, Maine, Maine Farmers Press, 1891.
Holbrook, Stewart W., *Holy Old Mackinaw*. New York, Macmillan Co., 1956.
————, *Yankee Exodus*. New York, Macmillan Co., 1950.
Yankee Logger. New York, International Paper Co., 1960.
Huntington, J.H., *Early History of Coos County in New Hampshire*. Concord, New Hampshire. Granite Monthly, 1879.
Josselyn, John, *New England Rarities*. London, G. Widdows, 1672.
Kilbourne, F.W., *Chronicles of the White Mountains*. Boston, Houghton, Mifflin, 1916.
Lapham and Maxim, *History of Paris, Maine*. Paris, Maine, Oxford Democratic, 1884.
Lapham, W.B., *History of Rumford, Maine*. Augusta, Maine, Maine Farmers Press, 1890.
Lawrance, Walter A., *Reports to the Androscoggin River Technical Committee*, 1961, 1963, 1965.
Leading Business Men of Lewiston, Augusta and Vicinity. Boston, Mercantile Pub. Co., 1889.
Leane, John J., *The Oxford Story*. New York, Oxford Paper Co., 1958.
Lewiston, City of, *Records of Referendum, April 15, 1876*.
Lewiston Water Power Co., *2nd Annual Report*. Boston, 1852.
Maine Reports, *Lewiston Steam Mill Co. vs Richardson Lake Dam Co*. Androscoggin County, 1883.
Maine Water Improvement Commission, *Reports, 1965-1966; Androscoggin River Classification, 1966; Little Androscoggin River Classification, 1966*.
Merrill, Georgia Drew, *History of Androscoggin County, Maine*. Boston, W.A. Furgussen & Co., 1891.
———— *History of Coos County, N.H.* Syracuse, New York, 1888.
Milne, Lorus J. and Margery, *Water and Life*, New York, Atheneum, 1964.
Monroe, Ira Thompson, *History of Livermore and Its Pioneers*. Lewiston Journal, 1928.
Muskie, Senator Edmund, *Reports* (1965-1966). Senate Sub-Committee on Water Pollution.
New England Interstate Water Pollution Control Commission, *Reports, 1955-1966*.
New Hampshire Water Pollution Commission, *Androscoggin River Tributaries – Staff Report No. 52* (1964); *Guide to Stream Classification, 1964*.
Palfrey, Jno. Gorham, *A Compendious History of N.E.* Boston, J.R. Osgood & Co., 1884.
Parrish, W.H., *Androscoggin County Art Work*. Chicago, 1893.
Parkman, Francis, *Jesuits of North America*. Boston, Little, Brown & Co., 1955.
———— *Pioneers of France in the New World*. Boston, Little, Brown & Co., 1955.
Peabody, Mrs. R.P., *History of Shelburne, N.H.* Gorham, New Hampshire, Mountaineer Print, 1882.
Peterson, Elmer, *Big Dam Foolishness*. New York, Devin-Adair, 1954
Powers, Grant, *Historical Sketches of the Discovery, Settlement & Progress of Events in the Coos Country & Vicinity*. Haverhill, J.F.C. Hayes, 1841.
Rumford Falls Power Co., *The Development of Rumford Falls*. Rumford, Maine, 1904.
Shaw, John O., *Bath, Brunswick and Richmond Directory*. Boston, J.O. Shaw, 1867.
Shezhan, H.V., *Diary-Aziscohos Dam Construction*. Union Water Power Co., 1909.
Sidio, A.D., *Report on Androscoggin River-N.H. & Maine*. Washington, D.C., U.S. Dept. of Health, Education and Welfare, 1962.
———— *Androscoggin River Basin, N.H. & Maine*. Washington, D.C., U.S. Dept. of Health, Education and Welfare, 1965.

Smith, Captain John, *A Description of New England (1620); Travels and Works; New England Trials* (1620). Auber Edition, 1884, J.S. Billings Memorial Collection of the New York Public Library.

Starbird, Charles M., *Indians of the Androscoggin Valley*. Lewiston, Maine, Lewiston Journal Print, 1928.

Dr. Nathaniel T. True. Augusta, Maine, Maine Farmers Press, 1892.

Turner, Augustus, *100th Anniversary - Lewiston, Me*. Auburn, Maine, Merrill & Weber, 1895.

Union Water Power Co., *Operations of Androscoggin River Water Storage System*. Boston, 1910.

U.S. Dept. of Health, Education & Welfare, Various bulletins on clean water issued between 1960 and 1966. Washington, D.C.

Wheeler, George A. and Henry W., *History of Brunswick, Topsham and Harpswell, Maine*. Boston, A. Mudge & Son.

Wiley, Benjamin G., *Incidents in White Mountain History*. Concord, New Hampshire, 1855.

Williamson, William D., *History of Maine*. Hallowell, Maine, Cogswell, 1832.

Wood, Richard G., *A History of Lumbering in Maine, 1820-1861*. University of Maine Press, 1961.

Wright, Congressman Jim, *The Coming Water Famine*. New York, Coward-McCann, 1966.

Archives, Letters and Unpublished Collections

Androscoggin Historical Society, Auburn, Maine, *Journal of Stephen Chase, 1772-1843*; miscellaneous correspondence and records.

Auburn Public Library, clippings of *Little Family*, George T. Little collection; private collections and correspondence.

Berlin, New Hampshire, Public Library, newspaper files of *The Berlin Reporter*, 1898-1966; Mrs. Mildred Kilgore of Gorham, New Hampshire, manuscript: *History of Gorham*, New Hampshire.

Lewiston Daily Sun and the *Lewiston Evening Journal*, files.

Maine Historical Society, Portland, Maine, James P. Baxter's Collected Papers; James Curtis' Journal, 1793-1830; *The Eastern Argus*, files, 1853; The Garcelon Family papers.

New York Public Library, Ford Collection; Edward, Anthony and Alfred W. Little, collection of autographed material; local history and biographical collections.

Pejepscot Historical Society, Brunswick, Maine, Charles Carroll's address on the 150th Anniversary of incorporation of Town of Brunswick; Charles C. Everett paper on the 150th Anniversary; miscellaneous private papers from citizens of Brunswick and Topsham.

Union Water Power Company, Lewiston, Maine, records and correspondence, 1836-1966.

LIST OF
PHOTOGRAPHS & MAPS

With a few notable exceptions, all the photographs included in this volume are by Roger Godbout, a native of Berlin, New Hampshire and sensitive to the moods of the valley . . . former U.S. Army photographer and practised professional . . . recipient of the New England Press Association's 1971-72 Photographer of the Year Award. The early photograph of "The Neck" on page 100 is from the collection of the late Victor Beaudoin, official photographer for Brown Company for many years. Those appearing on pages 104 and 128 are from the files of the Oxford Paper Company.

INDEX

174 / *Evolution of a Valley*